BRAVE DEEDS OF CONFEDERATE SOLDIERS

by

Philip Alexander Bruce
Author of "Robert E. Lee" and
"The Rise of the New South"

THE CONFEDERATE
REPRINT COMPANY
☆   ☆   ☆   ☆
WWW.CONFEDERATEREPRINT.COM

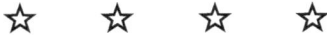

Brave Deeds of Confederate Soldiers
by Philip Alexander Bruce

Originally Published in 1916
by George W. Jacobs and Company
Philadelphia, Pennsylvania

Reprint Edition © 2014
The Confederate Reprint Company
Post Office Box 2027
Toccoa, Georgia 30577
www.confederatereprint.com

Cover and Interior Design by
Magnolia Graphic Design
www.magnoliagraphicdesign.com

ISBN-13: 978-0692294789
ISBN-10: 0692294783

FOREWORD

☆　　☆　　☆　　☆

In the composition of the present volume, I was indebted particulary to John Easten Cooke's *Wearing of the Gray*, and Col. Jennings C. Wise's *Military History of the Virginia Military Institute*, for the vivid impression which they gave me of the high, the gallant, and the romantic aspects of the Confederate Soldier's character. I was also indebted to Mr. W. H. Sargeant, of the Norfolk Public Library, for numerous courtesies that facilitated my use of the valuable collection of works relating to Confederate history now in his custody.

P. A. B.
Norfolk, Virginia
July 15, 1916

CONTENTS

☆   ☆   ☆   ☆

CHAPTER ONE
Military Influences in the Old Southern Life

☆　☆　☆　☆

If any one of my readers could have mounted into an aero-plane in 1860, and taken a flight from the Potomac to the Rio Grande, he would have found himself throughout his aerial jour-ney looking down upon a region on which nature had bestowed many striking features, but man only one. As he coursed along, he would have observed a land where agriculture alone had left a perceptible mark; but not such a mark, however, as to recall the well tilled countries of the Old World. The greater proportion of the landscape would have been seen to be overgrown with woods; open fields would have been discovered here and there on the uplands, and narrow belts of ground in cotton, tobacco, or corn along the banks of all the streams; here and there the roof of a planter's mansion would have been detected peeping above the foliage of the trees; or a yeoman's humbler house shining on a bare hillside; or the cabins of the slaves nestling in the shadow of barns and stables.

The spires of few large cities would have been seen, and only here and there the smoke from the chimneys of a country town. Still more rarely would lines of railway have been noticed. There were not enough of these lines to link up every corner of that almost boundless rural region. It is true that the great divi-sions of the South were united by the locomotive, but vast areas were still remote from all facilities for transportation except by steamboat or batteau; the principal means of getting about, not only from neighborhood to neighborhood, but not infrequently from one important town to another, consisted still of the riding horse and the carriage; and for the accommodation of their owners, there were comfortable though primitive inns or ordinaries at all the crossings of the principal public highways.

The seclusion of the whole region left a very deep impression on the disposition of its inhabitants. In a general way, it fostered in them a passionate, an almost romantic, love of the soil; a love that was further intensified by their descent as a body from the original settlers of that part of the Union; for this meant that they and their forbears had been associated with it for many generations. Indeed, time had brought about a complete identity of feeling, sentiment, and points of view even where the earliest population was sprung from different European nationalities. The fact too that the vast majority of the inhabitants had been engaged in the same calling for so long a period had brought to bear a powerful influence to give the final touch to this homogeneity, which was to do so much to bind the people of the South together throughout the war.

To a people like the Southern people, retired from the world at large, and in their family seats from each other also, home had a meaning far more sentimental than it has for a people who live in swarming cities, where a change of residence from one house or one street to another is a very common occurrence. Those homes in the Southern countrysides had, in most instances, come down from a distant past; they were invested with the sacred interest of ancestral traditions and personal association alike; and were expected to descend to a remote posterity of the same blood, who, in their turn, would look upon them with the same affection. This love of the family centre was shared by the small and large land-owner equally, and was one of the strongest ties that united all classes in the life of the general community.

It was this love of home, with its thronging recollections of the past both near and far – this clear vision of a house surrounded by ancient trees, perhaps, and standing in the midst of a wide rural domain, or of a few acres only – that nerved the arm of many a Southern soldier and strengthened his soul in repelling invasion. Love of the South was inextricably mixed up with this love of the family hearth, whether imposing or humble in character. Love of one particular spot, of one neighborhood, of one State, was the foundation stone of the love of the entire region which entered so deeply into the spirit of the Confederate soldier; and men who cared nothing whatever for the political causes of the war fought just as bravely as those who did, because they were animated by this intense local and sectional patriotism, which had been largely produced by the retired country life that they had led on their own inherited estates, whether great or small in area.

Another influence which more directly encouraged the military spirit arose from the fact that the people of the South, owing to their possession of the same economic and social system from the earliest Colonial times, only slightly changed by the adoption of a Republican form of government, were more keenly conscious of the traditions, customs, and habits of the historic past than the inhabitants of other parts of the Union, where there had been a vast industrial growth, a great accumulation of wealth, and a large addition of foreign citizens. Especially vivid was their recollection of the exploits of their fathers and grandsires in the different wars in which the United States had been engaged. By numerous firesides on plain and mountain as late as 1860, stirring tales were related of heroic conduct and poignant suffering during the incursions of the Indians along the Southern borders. Many a soldier still survived who had followed General Jackson to the battle of the Horseshoe, and General Taylor to the skirmishes of the Everglades; while all the way down the Alleghanies, from the Holston to the Alabama, there were still pointed out the scenes where the men in buckskin, with rifle in hand, had as pioneers fought the cunning savages waving the tomahawk and the scalping knife.

But the exploits of Marion and Sumter, Light Horse Harry Lee and Morgan, and many a local hero in the Revolutionary war, were narrated with still keener pride, and with quite as much familiarity as if those deeds of dazzling gallantry had been performed within the memory of the speakers. King's Mountain and the Cowpens were as well known in detail to the old men as to the brightest schoolboys, and added fuel to the patriotic ardour and the military spirit that were felt in mansion and log house alike. The victories of the Mexican campaigns were events of yesterday, and few Southern counties were unable to boast of a veteran who had marched in the ranks under Scott or Taylor. Many a newly built home beneath the Southern oaks and magnolias bore the name of Monterey, Resaca, Montevideo, Buena Vista or Montezuma. Daredevil expeditions like those which the filibuster Walker, as brilliant an adventurer as Aaron Burr, led against Central America, aroused the warmest sympathy and enthusiasm in the South, where their largest number of volunteers were obtained, because there so many men were animated by an irrepressible thirst for dangerous enterprises.

It was due to this universal love of adventure – this hunger for an active and stirring life – that Sir Walter Scott enjoyed such extraordinary popularity in the homes of the Southern people. There were few libraries of importance among them that were lacking in those splendid volumes in which he has drawn such romantic pictures of the entrenched camp, the martial council, and the sombre castle swarming to the battlements with mail-clad defenders; or has described so vividly the headlong charges and the sword-to-sword clashes of the battlefield; or related so graphically the adventures of wandering soldiers of fortune in Highland glen or on the plains of France and Palestine.

It was due to this military spirit, which found such pleasure in the books of the great Scottish novelist, that the tournament remained down to the beginning of the war one of the most popular kinds of amusement in the South. It is true that this sport did not take the ancient form of a personal combat between knights-at-arm, but for clear sight, firm nerves, skillful horsemanship, and sheer physical strength, the tilting in a Southern field was almost as keen a test as the tilting in the lists of the Middle Ages.

The prevalence of the duello was another indication of the existence of the military spirit. It was considered by the gentlemen of the South to be the proper method of settling every bitter altercation which had ended in a personal insult, while with the lower orders of society in the same communities the duello usually took the form of a violent brawl, in which blood was apt to be shed without regard to the etiquette of the code. Men were aware that they would be held responsible in the duelling field for slander and calumny; and they also knew that they would be branded as cowards should they refuse a challenge.

A more rational influence in encouraging the military spirit was the necessity imposed on the men in the secluded plantation houses of the South to defend the women and children of their families against possible attack or intrusion. Not only were these homes generally in a retired situation, but they were nearly always surrounded by numerous slaves, who, however peaceable they might appear to be, yet at any time might rise in revolt. There were no policemen at the next crossroads, who, by a blast upon a horn, could be summoned at once to give aid in putting down an insurrection. The fathers, the sons, and the husbands never for a moment forgot the vital fact that their own strong arms must be relied on first of all to save those dear to them from every kind of outrage, whether threatened by freemen or bondsmen; and this responsibility they did not fail to meet with a resolute spirit whenever they were faced by it.

The military tendency was further encouraged by the zealous interest with which the muster had always been regarded throughout the South. In some measure, this was due to the presence of so many slaves. At regular intervals, every man capable of bearing arms was required to repair to a field, which, for many years, perhaps, had been chosen for the drilling. Here he and his companions were put through a series of manœuvres; and, however uncouth and awkward they might show themselves to be, they at least were animated by the true spirit of patriotic soldiers. These musters had been begun in early Colonial times, and they continued to be held down to the outbreak of the Civil War. They formed an instructive episode in the life of the community, for, by subjecting the men of the proper age to occasional military discipline on a peaceful arena, it prepared them, in some degree, for the stern duties of real battlefields.

These occasions were generally made more distinguished, if not more informative, by the presence of a veteran officer, who had won a high reputation in some previous war. Whether a mere looker-on or a participant in the exercises, his share in the event gave it a more serious meaning from a military point of view at least. There were other influences, which less directly but not less thoroughly trained Southern men to play from the very beginning a vigorous part in the fighting on the battlefield, or in the marches that preceded or followed each conflict. For instance, the routine of their main occupation, agriculture, had a tendency to encourage in them a manly and hardy spirit because it required them to spend most of their time out of doors. They were unaccustomed to the inactive and sedentary employments of shop and factory, or to the sheltered existence of city pavements and tenements; their eyes, except at night, rested almost uninterruptedly on the open fields, the massive forests, the unrolled canopy of the sky; they were familiar with every aspect of the landscape as the hours of light and darkness passed over it, and with every mark which the different seasons left on hill and vale and plain. Constant and prolonged exposure had hardened their frames to every sort of weather – the driving rains of spring, the exhausting heats of summer, the chill blasts and blinding snows of winter – all had been faced and breasted with a spirit that was unconscious of discouragement or depression. Whether they were on foot or on horseback, they withstood nature's buffetings with an unshaken equanimity, for such vicissitudes were but the ordinary experiences of their daily lives; they knew the fields, the woods, and the streams in the vicinity of their dwelling houses as thoroughly as the scholar knows his books; and they felt as much at home in the most remote and secluded spots as they did in the chambers and halls of their own mansions, or in the narrow rooms of their own log cabins.

The principal diversions of the Southern people were, with

few exceptions, associated with this life in the open air, and partook of its free and manly nature. They had a particular fondness for hunting. Now to be a hunter is the first step to being a warrior. The wary aboriginal Indian, wandering through the primeval forests, was hunter and warrior at the same time; and it was the skill with bow and arrow acquired as a hunter – it was the craft that he had learned as a woodsman – which enabled him to carry off so many bloody scalps as a warrior. The huntsmen among the Southern people were not to be counted for their number. There were few young men who could recall the years of their earliest youth when they were unable at least to shoot off a gun. The father, returning home after a day passed in the stubble fields beating up partridges, rarely failed to require the small son, perhaps not ten years of age, to discharge his fowling piece; and should the little fellow be severely kicked, he was not permitted afterwards to show any fear when ordered to shoot a second time. Every mansion boasted of many guns of different sizes, and every log cabin of at least one, however ancient the pattern; and none were kept simply to ornament the trophy-covered walls, whether built of stone or common logs.

The accuracy of the aim of these huntsmen was as perfect as long experience by flood and field could make it. The vastness and variety of the region of country which they tramped or rode over assured them all kinds of game ranging from the smallest to the largest. Birds and animals alike teemed in number. The long line of seacoast was haunted by flocks of ducks, geese, swan, and plover; the plain between the ocean and the Alleghanies by partridges, snipe, woodcock, wild turkeys, pigeons, and doves; and the mountains by deer, bear, and wildcat. Each season offered a special form of sport; and few forms failed to call for the possession of strength of body, keenness of eye, and patience of spirit in their successful pursuit. These qualities were especially required in the chase of the wild turkey, bear, raccoon, and fox.

The vast Southern forests were frequented by numerous flocks of turkeys, one of the wildest and wariest of game birds, and only to be killed by the exercise of cunning and caution, and by the most unwearied energy on the part of the hunter. This was the school in which some of the most famous scouts of the Southern armies learned their art of successfully following up the enemy.

There was far more danger in the pursuit of the bear, which was found in the swamps and canebrakes of the lowlands as well as in the remotest mountains. Many hours were passed in the forests in the search for it; the parties camped out at night; and the hunt was kept up all day without regard to the roughness of the country.

A taste for life in the open air, indifference to personal risks, and forgetfulness of continuous physical exertion, were also instilled by the pursuit of the raccoon, although in itself a harmless animal. It is true that the only danger in such a pursuit arose entirely from the darkness, in consequence of which casualties from falling trees, snakebites, and plunging into deep bogs were likely to occur; but the hunters were always drawn far into the woods, and thus learned to know the forest as well under its nocturnal appearance as under its aspect during the day.

Still more productive of a bold spirit and vigorous frame was the sport of fox hunting, which was popular in all parts of the South with every class in the community. The wild gallop with horns and hounds over the rough face of the country, with its hills and valleys, bare fields, and thick woods; the continuation of the pursuit from the gray of the morning until a late hour in the night, and its frequent resumption at dawn for a second day's run; the indifference to the character of the weather in the enjoyment of the sport – all this was excellent practice for fitting the young men for the requirements of service in the cavalry.

The universal love of the horse in the South, and its constant use for recreation or display, was also promotive of the military spirit. As from childhood almost every boy knew how to shoot a gun, so from the time he had the length of leg to bestride a saddle, he was able to ride. While still a little fellow, he would perch up behind the negro stable-man when the horses were taken to water in the morning or at night; and he soon acquired sufficient confidence to ride his own pony, the first step to mounting a larger animal.

Before the Civil War, most of the Southern boys obtained the rudiments of their education in what was known as the old field school because situated in some retired spot equally distant from the different homes in the neighborhood. Very often, the only way of reaching this school was by a narrow bridle path through the woods. Hither came the boys on horseback five mornings of the week in all sorts of weather, at every season of the year; nor were they always content to let their steeds walk or jog quietly along – many a race was run under the bower of forest leaves, in which skill was necessary to avoid the trunks of trees that sprang up along either side of the way.

There were numerous other opportunities of becoming proficient in the art of riding; every Saturday was a holiday, and from morning until darkness came on, the boys were using their horses either in hunting in the fields and forests or in traveling to some distant mill-pond famous far and wide for perch and mullet. Every one of them looked upon himself as fully able to break in a young colt however raw and fractious it may have come from the pasture; and many a young fellow was seriously injured by his reckless indifference to the dangers of mounting such a wild beast before its spirit had been even partially broken.

This knowledge of horseflesh, this love of equestrian exercise, was never lost by the Southerner, however old he might grow. Though he might be poor in a property sense, it was not often that he did not own at least one horse, which served both as his helper in working the tobacco lots and cotton fields, and as his carrier in visiting neighbors, attending church, or moving about the countryside on business. He rode to the distant county seat to be present at the sessions of court; and it was on horseback too that he traveled to political barbecues and religious camp meetings. There was no public occasion in his life, indeed, which did not permit of this means of locomotion; in fact, at certain seasons of the year, the roads were hardly passable with ease except by persons on horseback; and this custom led many women to acquire the like skill so that they might not be impeded in getting about their neighborhoods.

The planters took great pride in the pure blood of their horses; skilled attention was everywhere given to horse breeding; and universal interest was felt in racing. Many large estates possessed a private course laid off with more or less exactness; there was a public track in nearly every county, where trials of speed came off each year, with crowds of people in attendance; while one of the principal features of every agricultural fair was the succession of heats run by horses that enjoyed a reputation for fleetness throughout that part of the South.

With all this knowledge of horseflesh and skill in horsemanship, was it strange that the Southern States should have produced so many brilliant cavalry leaders during the Civil War? The fact had been noted from the first years of the West Point Military Academy that the cadets appointed from the districts between the Potomac and the Rio Grande were especially proficient in horsemanship as a part of their course of study; and they were thus accomplished because they had been brought up to love horses and had become expert long before they were leaping the hurdles in the riding school on the Hudson. The cavalry was the favorite arm of the Confederate service; the arm which all would have preferred to join; the one arm for which even the soldiers in the infantry had been trained in the first great essential by constant previous exercise at their own homes. Wheeler, Fitzhugh Lee, Hampton, Forrest, and Stuart were the most famous officers of the cavalry corps, but behind those gallant cavaliers, there rode thousands of men, not only fully as gallant as they were, but also from their earliest boyhood just as deeply versed in horsemanship. Again and again, in the midst of flying bullets, while the musketry was crackling and the cannon reverberating to the sky, the song rang out gaily from many a brave lip: "If you wish to have a good time, come jine the cavalry." That song was the favorite air of Stuart, who summed up in his dashing and chivalrous personality, not only the finest qualities of the fearless and stainless soldier, but also the boldest characteristics of a horseman who has passed almost his entire life in the saddle.

CHAPTER TWO
Belle Boyd the Spy

☆　☆　☆　☆

During the early months of the war, the lower valley of the Shenandoah was the scene of unusual activity on the part of Southern spies, whose zealousness was very much encouraged by the conditions which prevailed there throughout that period. First, the people living in this corner of Virginia were almost fanatically loyal to the Confederate Government, and they were so, not only because the most influential citizens were descended from the oldest families in the State, but, above all, because persons of every class had been violently alarmed and embittered by the John Brown Raid, which, had it succeeded, would have plunged them into all the horrors of a slave insurrection.

In the second place, the entire region was constantly passing from the hands of the Confederates under the control of the Federals or the reverse. Now the Northern army would advance from Harper's Ferry as far as Winchester and Front Royal; then the Southern would suddenly face about and drive them back, and in their turn take possession of these towns; which, in a short time, would be abandoned, only to be reoccupied by the Federal troops. One week, a family would find their home subject to the daily inspection of the Federal provost-marshal; the next they would be receiving friendly visits from distinguished Confederate officers.

In the light of the local devotion to the Confederate cause, and also of these opportunities to collect and report information of high value from a military point of view, it was natural that there should be spies in every neighborhood, who would be furtively engaged in transmitting such information to General Jackson, who was opposing the Federal armies in that part of Virginia.

The most famous of all these spies was Belle Boyd, the daughter of a Confederate officer, who was the head of a wealthy and widely connected family residing at Martinsburg, a town situated not far from Harper's Ferry. She was just seventeen years of age when the war broke out and had only recently left the schoolroom. Beautiful, intelligent, and high-spirited, and passionately loyal to the Confederate cause, she was as cool in courage and as firm in purpose as the bravest soldier on the battlefield.

When General Shields occupied Front Royal, he took possession of the home of Belle Boyd's grandmother, who resided there, and made it his headquarters. There was a small cottage within the enclosure, and to this the members of the family, among them Belle Boyd herself, withdrew. Having become an object of suspicion to the Federal authorities in Martinsburg by their seizure of a letter which she was about to send to General Jackson, she found herself so closely watched there that she decided to visit her relations in Front Royal. She soon got on an easy and friendly footing with the Federal commander, a genial Irishman, and took advantage of her constant association with him and his officers, to pick up information of importance. Committing it to paper from day to day, she dispatched note after note to the Confederate leaders by means of a messenger on whose fidelity she knew she could rely. She did not always use a cypher, and made no effort to conceal her handwriting. After some time so taken up, she concluded that she could further aid the Confederate cause by going in person to Richmond.

"General," she said to General Shields as soon as she saw him again, "I want you to give me a passport to Richmond."

General Shields laughed at her for making such a request, and indulged in a good deal of badinage at her expense.

"Old Jackson's army," he said, "is so demoralized that I

I dare not trust you to their tender mercies. I will annihilate those rebels in a few days, and then you can go where you choose."

General Shields had now determined to advance and attack the Confederate army encamped at a point further south. The night before he set his troops in motion, he held a council of war at his headquarters in the Boyd residence. Belle Boyd, who had been daily passing backward and forwards between the mansion and the cottage without being questioned, had frequently visited a bedroom, well known to her, situated just above the apartment where the council was to meet, which happened to be the drawing room of the house. In rummaging about the closet, she had noticed a hole in the floor, through which the sound of voices in the room underneath could be easily heard. Indeed, it was so large, that, placing her eye over it, she could without difficulty make out any person who might be seated below.

The night the council came together, she was talking with some of the officers in the drawing room, and finding that a council was about to be held, she retired, but instead of leaving the house and going over to the cottage, she quietly ascended the stairs to the bedroom, and entering the closet, and lying down flat on the floor, she placed her ear at the hole and distinctly caught every word uttered by the men assembled around the table below. The discussion did not come to an end until one o'clock in the morning, but during the long hours it was carried on, she did not change her position.

The council broke up and the officers withdrew from the house to their own quarters. When silence had again fallen, Belle Boyd stole from the closet, descended the stairs on tiptoe, unbolted the door without noise, and passed with quiet steps across the threshold to the yard without. On reaching her own room in the cottage, she took down in cypher the information about the Federal plans which she had just obtained. Without resting a moment or securing a morsel of food, she ran to the stable, and leading out and saddling one of the horses, mounted and rode off at a gallop towards the nearest mountains.

Fortunately for her, she had not forgotten to bring with her several passports which she had asked of General Shields to enable some of her Confederate friends to get through the lines. She had not gone far when she was challenged by a Federal sentinel, and was only permitted to continue her journey after her passport had been shown and examined. This happened to her several times, until, having left all the pickets behind, she was at liberty to ride on without further interruption.

In order to be more secure, she deserted the road and entered the fields, through which she moved rapidly in spite of the darkness. She had covered fifteen miles of ground when she found herself in front of the house of a friend whom she had often visited. Not a single light was to be seen in any of the windows owing to the lateness of the hour. Leaping from her saddle, and not stopping even to tie her horse, she ran up the steps, and with the butt of her whip pounded violently on the door. No response was made to the blows at first.

"Is it possible," she thought to herself, "that there is nobody at home!"

She knocked more vigorously. She called. Then a voice was heard from the depths within:

"Who is there?"

"It is I."

"But who are you? What is your name?"

"Belle Boyd. I have important intelligence to communicate to Colonel Ashby. Is he here?"

"Wait a minute, I will come down."

When the person who had been speaking opened the door, his first question was, "How on earth did you get here?"

"Oh, I forced the sentries. But I have no time to talk. Tell me where Colonel Ashby is to be found?"

Hardly had she spoken when a door suddenly opened and Colonel Ashby himself stood before her.

"Good God, Miss Belle," he exclaimed, when he recognized her, "where did you come from? Have you dropped from the clouds? Or am I dreaming?"

"You are awake and I am not an angel from heaven," she

replied laughingly; and then quickly becoming serious again, she repeated to him all that she had overheard of the decisions arrived at by the council. She handed him the memorandum in cypher, which she knew he was able to translate, and mounting her jaded horse, bade the dashing Confederate officer, who had not yet fully recovered from his astonishment, a gay farewell and started on her return through the fields by which she had come. After a ride of two hours, she reached the neighborhood of the town, where there was danger of her being stopped and arrested by the sentinels; but she ran only upon one, and he was so fast asleep that she succeeded in galloping by him before he could shake off his slumber and raise his gun to shoot. Having unsaddled and fed her faithful horse, she turned into bed just as dawn began to break. That day, General Shields, at the head of his troops, left Front Royal in search of Jackson, with the unsuccessful result that is recorded in history.

After the departure of the Federal army, Belle Boyd applied for a passport that would permit her and a cousin to visit Winchester. The passport was promised by the provost-marshal, but when the carriage rolled up to the door next morning, the document had not been sent by him; and it was reported that he had left town on a scouting expedition. A Federal lieutenant whom they knew came to where the ladies were impatiently waiting.

"You profess to be a great friend of mine," said Belle Boyd to him, "now prove it. Pass us through the pickets."

The young officer hesitated a moment; then bidding them enter the carriage, promised that he would accompany them the entire way to assure their safety. Arriving in Winchester, the whole party decided to remain there over night. Some hours before they were to leave next morning, a gentleman came to the house where the ladies were stopping. Handing two packages of letters to Belle Boyd, he said to her, "Will you see that these packages are got through the lines to the Confederate army in the Valley? This package (pointing to one of the two) is of great importance. The other is trifling in comparison."

Taking from his pocket a small note, "This," he said, "is an important paper also. Please endeavor to have it forwarded to General Jackson. Do you understand?"

"I do," she replied, "I will obey your order promptly and implicitly."

The most important package she concealed about the person of her negro maid, as she was confident that a black woman would not be searched. The other one she dropped into a small basket which she was taking with her. On it she had written, "By the kindness of Lieutenant H." She hid the note in her own bosom.

She decided that, before she should set out, it would be more prudent to obtain a passport from the officer in command of Winchester, Colonel Fillebrowne, which would enable her to return safely to Front Royal whether Lieutenant H. should accompany her or not. How was she to secure it? Was she not the notorious rebel spy, Belle Boyd? She went to a florist who had a shop nearby, and purchasing a very handsome bouquet, sent it, "with her best wishes," to the Federal commander; and she accompanied it with the request that he would allow her, by his express order, to return to her relatives in Front Royal. The passport was promptly dispatched to her, with a polite letter, in which "the dear lady" was thanked for "so sweet a compliment." Lieutenant H. having now joined the cousins and their maid, all started together on the return journey. On arriving at the picket line, two determined looking men stopped the carriage. They were really detectives.

"We have been instructed," said one of them looking through the window at Belle Boyd, "to arrest you."

"For what?" she boldly inquired.

"You are charged with carrying letters of importance to the enemy," was the reply.

The coachman was ordered to turn the carriage around and drive back to Winchester. The two detectives rode on either side of the vehicle all the way. When the party entered the office at headquarters, the cousin and the maid almost sank to the floor with fright, but Belle Boyd showed no discomposure whatever.

"Have you any letters about you," was the first question

put to her by the provost-marshal in his sternest voice. Feeling sure that she would be searched should she answer in the negative, she simply stooped down and took from her basket the package on which she had written the words: "By the kindness of Lieutenant H.," and handed it to the officer with a low bow, but without uttering a word.

"'By the kindness of Lieutenant H!'" he exclaimed in angry tones when he had read the superscription, "what does this mean? Have you any other packages or letters?"

"Look for yourself," replied Belle Boyd coolly, and she turned the basket upside down so that its contents fell in confusion to the floor. Lieutenant H's face suddenly blanched, for he remembered that he had a second package, which Belle Boyd had taken from the maid and given to him while the carriage was on its way back to Winchester. He drew it from his pocket and placed it on the table; to his consternation, this package also was inscribed with the words "By the kindness of Lieutenant H." When opened, it was found to contain copies of a newspaper which would have conveyed to the Confederates information of great value. In vain both Belle Boyd and the Lieutenant asserted that he knew nothing of the character of its contents when the package was delivered to him; the provost-marshal looked at her sternly and took no notice of the disclaimers of herself and her companion.

"What note is that you have in your hand?" he demanded.

"This little scrap of paper?" said Belle Boyd innocently. "You can have it if you want it. It is nothing. Here it is." She appeared to be about to hand it to him, but in reality she had made up her mind to swallow it. Just as she was about to raise it to her mouth to do so, the provost-marshal's attention was diverted to his subordinate, and he forgot, in his renewed indignation over that officer's supposed treasonable conduct, the existence of the important letter to Jackson, which was almost within his grasp. The curious manner in which Lieutenant H. was involved in the transmission of the packages alone saved Belle Boyd from the punishment that would have certainly followed from her possessing such compromising documents.

A few days afterwards, she was sitting in her room at Front Royal quietly reading to her cousin and grandmother, when her negro maid rushed in.

"Oh, Miss Belle," she exclaimed, "I tink de rebels are a comin' for de Yankees am makin' an awful fuss in de streets."

Belle Boyd sprang to the window. The servant was right – the street was in a state of great confusion; men were shouting and vehicles were jammed together. There was plainly some extraordinary cause for alarm.

"What is the matter?" she called to a Federal officer whom she knew as she saw him passing.

"The Confederates under General Jackson are approaching," he replied. "They are driving back the pickets and are now within a mile of the town. We are trying to get the ordnance and quartermaster's stores out of their reach."

"But what will you do with the stores in the large depot?" asked Belle Boyd.

"Burn them, of course," replied the officer. "If the rebels come up too quickly for us to do so, we will fight as long as we can, and if defeated, retreat to Winchester, where we will join General Banks. We will burn all the bridges behind us."

It happened that, at this moment. Belle Boyd was in the possession of the following military facts known only to the Federals: General Banks was stationed at Strasburg with four thousand men; General White could quickly march up to Winchester from Harper's Ferry and reinforce the Federal troops in that town; Shields and Geary were posted not far below Front Royal; while Fremont had not yet arrived in the Valley. How was she to send this information to General Jackson? The note received at Winchester had also to be forwarded to him. If he failed to get both, he might fall into the trap which the combined Federal commanders had set for his destruction. All were to converge to catch his army in their coils.

She went to the drawer and took out a pair of opera glasses which she kept there, and through these she could plainly descry the Confederate vanguard approaching at a distance of three-quarters of a mile. There was no time for her to lose if she was to communicate with Jackson. Descending to the lower floor in great haste and opening the front door of the house, she saw standing on the pavement a small group of men who had often spoken in her presence of their devotion to the cause of the South. Beckoning them to her side, she said in a low voice, "Will any one of you carry to General Jackson information I have collected which may save his army?"

They positively refused to undertake so dangerous a mission. "You go, you go," they cried out as if with one voice.

Perceiving that she would gain nothing by importuning them, she turned and went back into the house determined to carry the message herself, in spite of the perils which she knew she would have to face. Having put on a white sunbonnet, she went into the street, and as she passed down it on her way to the road leading in the direction from which Jackson was approaching, she had to meet the questioning gaze of hundreds of Federal soldiers; but as the town was still in a state of great disorder, no one stopped her to inquire about the purpose of her movements, although she was as much as ever under the ban of suspicion. Leaving Front Royal behind, she decided to turn from the road into the open fields in the hope that she would be able to conceal herself there until the Confederate troops should come up and protect her. There was, however, not enough cover to hide her from the eye, especially as she was wearing a white apron over a dark blue dress; and her bonnet also was of the same conspicuous color. She could, in reality, be easily seen at a very considerable distance.

All this time she could hear the loud firing that was going on between the two hostile forces. The Federal artillery had taken position on a height that commanded the whole length of the road along which the Confederate army was advancing to the attack, while a large body of Federal infantry had made a fortress of the hospital, and were pouring a heavy fusillade of musketry from its windows. This was responded to hotly from the Confederate side, and the din was rapidly increasing in intensity. The Federal pickets, outnumbered, began to fall back, and as they did so, they saw

Belle Boyd running across the fields and they opened fire on her. Balls soon were hitting the ground about her feet and passing alarmingly close to her head. The Federal soldiers in the hospital followed the example of the pickets, and in a few minutes Belle Boyd's clothes were pierced by bullets in several places, but fortunately for herself, she was not struck in the body.

To increase the perils of her situation, many of the shells in the cross fire between the Federal and the Confederate batteries, burst over her and scattered their fragments in every direction. Suddenly a Federal shell came to the ground within twenty feet of where in her bewilderment she had momentarily stopped, but she had the presence of mind to throw herself flat on the earth before it exploded; and when it did so, she was covered with the flying dirt which it raised. Leaping to her feet immediately after the concussion she ran forward at the top of her speed, while the musket balls still hurtled about her and the shells continued to scream in the air overhead. She felt that, not only was she in imminent danger of being killed, but also her death might mean the complete entrapment of the Confederate army. Through the open fields she almost flew, and when she came to a fence that stood in her way she threw herself over it with the agility of an athlete.

Not long after leaving the fence behind, she caught sight of the gray Confederate ranks, and she began at once waving her bonnet alternately towards them and towards the town. In response, the troops raised a loud cheer, and with a quickened step continued their advance, and as they went by her, a second cheer, louder than the first, broke from their throats.

"Were these all the forces which General Jackson could bring to the attack?" she asked herself in consternation, as she saw the men move past the spot on which she was standing. It was impossible for so few to outmatch the Federal armies in the neighborhood of Front Royal. Had she made the night ride to Colonel Ashby's, and was she now exposing herself to such peril, simply to lure these gallant men to their certain destruction by a superior foe?

She was so overcome that, sinking to her knees, she ut-

The Federal rear guard had just crossed over.

tered a fervent prayer for their deliverance. Rising from the ground, she saw to her great relief the main body of the Confederate forces emerge from behind a hill, which had, up to that time, hidden them from her sight. As the van approached, she was recognized by an officer who was a friend and connection of her family. Major Douglas of the Maryland line.

"Good God, Belle," he exclaimed as he rode up. "You here! What in the name of Heaven do you want?"

"Oh, Harry," she gasped, "give me time to get my breath!"

Having recovered her breath, she imparted as quickly as possible all the information which she had been able to gather about the positions of the Federal troops; and also handed to him the note which she had received in Winchester. She urged that the cavalry should be sent forward at once to seize all the bridges over the Shenandoah below the town before they could be destroyed, as she had been told they would be, by the withdrawing Federals. Major Douglas returned to General Jackson at a gallop to report what he had heard, and in a short time, Jackson, accompanied by Douglas, rode up, and having questioned her closely, offered her a horse and military escort to insure her getting back safely to town.

The cavalry reached the first bridge barely in time, the Federal rear guard had just crossed over and had already lighted the match which was to explode the heavy charges that had been placed under the stone arches. The other bridges were also saved by equal promptness. When Belle Boyd arrived at her home, the main Confederate army was filing through the streets, and as they caught sight of her on her doorstep, they raised a cheer in her honor. Although they were greatly exhausted, they pressed on in the track of the retreating Federals towards Winchester; Banks was compelled to withdraw to the other side of the Potomac; and the whole plan of the Federal campaign was thrown into confusion.

Two incidents are recorded which show how clearly the officers on either side recognized the importance of the information which Belle Boyd had either given herself or conveyed for others for the guidance of the Confederate leaders.

When the Confederate army, following up General Banks, approached Winchester, Colonel Fillebrowne, who, as we have seen, was in command there, began very hastily to gather together all his effects, and whilst he was doing this, a Southern friend of Belle Boyd entered the room.

"Colonel," he exclaimed, "how on earth did you get into this trap? Did you not know that Jackson was advancing?"

Colonel Fillebrowne pointed to the bouquet on the table which Belle Boyd had sent him only a few days before.

"That bouquet," said he sadly, "did all the mischief. The donor of that gift is responsible for all this misfortune."

The other incident which represents the reverse side of the shield, was the reception by her of the following note:

Miss Belle Boyd,

I thank you for myself and for the army for the immense service that you have rendered your country today.
Hastily, I am your Friend,

T. J. Jackson, C.S.A.

CHAPTER THREE
Up in a Baloon

☆　　☆　　☆　　☆

In the spring of 1862, General Magruder, who commanded that part of the Confederate forces known as the Army of the Peninsula, expecting a Federal assault from Old Point, threw up a formidable line of breastworks all the way from Yorktown to the margin of James river. The course selected for this line gave the entrenchments additional strength, for it followed the trend of certain outstanding physical features of that region, such as streams, swamps, and millponds, by which its surface was very much varied.

General McClellan, advancing his troops by land from the toe of the Peninsula, their flanks being protected by gunboats moving up the waters of the York and the James, was suddenly brought squarely up against this strong artificial barrier, with its natural buttresses, and was compelled to come to an abrupt halt.

This barrier was made still more impregnable by the arrival of General Johnston, with fresh forces to further man their whole length. Johnston, as the officer of highest rank on the ground, took the supreme control of the entire body of Confederate troops present. He pitched his headquarters some distance back from the banks of York river on a site that lay on very low ground, like the rest of the coastal region to which that part of the Peninsula belonged. Had there been a hill near at hand he could easily have observed, through a field glass, the dispositions of the soldiers in the enemy's encampments and the movements of the gunboats reconnoitering in the broad waters of the two neighboring rivers.

But there was no such height. The entire country, spread out on a dead level just a few feet above the reach of the waves at high tide, was simply a great plain formed at first of the sediment of the ocean bed. It was now overgrown with forests, chiefly of oak and pine, broken here and there by clearings under tillage for wheat or corn, or by pastures for cattle. The top of a tree afforded only a limited scope for the gaze of one peering out over the face of the landscape, since other trees, near or distant, obstructed the freedom of expanse. Indeed, the encampments of the Federals beyond the line of breastworks were really encircled by woods, and unless the eye of the Confederate observer could look directly down on them, it would have been impossible to ascertain their precise position, except possibly by the wreaths of smoke, which might, at certain hours, be rising from the fires of the field kitchens.

Nor could the wariest and most energetic scout be justly expected to report accurately as to the number of the Federal troops, or as to their exact disposition, since one man, or even half a dozen men, however experienced, would have found it impracticable to cover furtively the whole intricate field of the enemy's operations which had to be inspected and fully comprehended.

It was, however, imperative that the Confederate Commander should obtain information of what was going on beyond the line of breastworks. Were the enemy getting ready for an assault, and, if so, in what strength? When, as indicated by their movements, was the attack likely to be made? Johnston was entirely in the dark on these points at a moment when he wished to know positively the immediate intentions of the Federals as revealed by the actions of their troops in camp. There was little use in sending out a scout, as has been seen, for not only was the field to be reported on too broad, but he might be captured and never return. Nor was there any advantage, as already pointed out, in establishing a crow's nest in a tall pine, since no outlook was to be obtained thereby. How then was the General to surmount the disconcerting situation facing him?

Fortunately, when he set out for the Peninsula, he knew the general character of the country in which he was to campaign. What was the best means of seeing far and wide over this flat and jungle-like region? By a balloon, of course, Johnston had brought with him all the material for just such aircraft, and he now determined to put it to immediate use. This balloon, which, it is said, was the first that the Confederates employed, was made, not of rubber, stuff with difficulty procured in the South at that hour, but of thick cotton cloth, rendered very stiff and perfectly air tight by several coatings of tar. In ordinary times, the hydrogen gas with which to inflate the envelope would have been produced on the spot; but there were no facilities for doing this in a temporary Confederate camp, and, in consequence, hot air had to be used as a substitute.

Possessing a balloon, and with the means to make it rise from the ground into the sky, the General was now at a loss as to how to obtain an aeronaut who would be able to manage it safely. It was not sufficient that the man should have had some experience, and that he should possess an iron nerve; he should be a person too who could give an intelligent description of the dispositions of the hostile forces on land and water. Not only would he have to observe all that lay beneath him, but also make notes of what he saw so as to assure the most complete accuracy in his subsequent report to headquarters.

There was no one in the Confederate army present who had received any training at all as an air pilot; but this fact, though known to General Johnston, failed to discourage him, for it could be met in a measure by attaching the balloon to the ground by a long rope. It is true that the rope might be shot to pieces by the enemy's batteries when the balloon was up in the sky, but this was a risk which he knew would be taken by any brave man.

The General made his choice on a mere venture. Without stating the character of the task which he had in view, he wrote General Magruder to send to him a soldier who was familiar with this particular region of country by his having resided in it; who was a quick and shrewd observer; and whose courage was not likely to be shaken by his being placed in a dangerous and novel situation.

This note passed through the Adjutant-General's office, and was there read by a young fellow twenty-one years of age, John Randolph Bryan, who bore a name of social and political distinction in both Georgia and Virginia. Having been born in Gloucester county, which was situated on York river just opposite Yorktown, he had, from boyhood, known minutely the typography of the country now occupied by the two opposing armies; thus he possessed the first of the qualifications which the Commander had required; and as he was very anxious to win distinction, he ventured to think that he would not be found devoid of the others should he be put to the practical test by circumstances. He, therefore, requested General Magruder to assign him for whatever enterprise General Johnston had under consideration.

When Bryan set out for the latter's headquarters, he was ordered to report to the Commander in person. As he entered the General's tent, the General got his first sight of him and started back in undisguised astonishment at his aeronaut's youthful appearance. This surprise perhaps caused him to make his questions so keen and searching; indeed, his inquiries were put so sharply and so quickly as almost to disconcert the young man, cool and sturdy as he was.

"Have you any military knowledge, Sir? How long have you served in the army, Sir? If you were inspecting from a distance, Sir, would you be able to distinguish artillery from infantry, or infantry from dismounted cavalry? What information, Sir, have you about the different roads, creeks, and fords in this part of the Peninsula?"

These questions having been answered to his apparent satisfaction, he turned abruptly to his aide, who had been present during the interview. "Assign Mr. Bryan to the balloon service," he ordered. "He is expected to make at once the necessary reconnoissances. Please instruct him as to the precise information

Bryan was to use a small flag in signalling

which we shall want, and as to the form of the report which he will have to submit on his return from his flight."

Now Bryan was as brave as a young lion in spirit, and he also thirsted for a chance to win distinction for himself, but it had not occurred to him, when he volunteered his services, that his new career of adventure was to take him into the unstable regions of the upper air.

"General," he protested, "I never saw a balloon in my life. I know nothing. Sir, as to the proper way of managing one."

General Johnston looked at him sternly.

"What I want, Sir," he said in his briefest manner, "is a man to go up in the balloon. Hold yourself in readiness to obey my orders."

No room was left for further argument. Bryan withdrew somewhat shaken by the prospect of soon finding himself in the most novel situation of his life; but he resolved to face its dangers with the brave front which had always distinguished him. He felt just as a man who had never been in the water would do if ordered to throw himself overboard and swim to the shore. He was not aware at the moment he was informed of the task before him that the balloon would be attached to the ground; but while this would require of him less skill as an aeronaut, it would not really diminish his peril from shot and shell, for the balloon would still be a target for the enemy's batteries.

The hour having arrived for the ascension, he was escorted to the spot where the balloon was tied to a tree It had already been inflated with hot air by means of a flue that had sucked the air up from a roaring fire fed with pine knots and balls of turpentine. The rope that held down the huge envelope was at least half a mile in length, but was easily worked by the men in charge of it by drawing it around a windlass. The balloon could thus be made to ascend or descend at will.

Before entering the basket, Bryan was handed a small flag which he was told to use in signaling to the men at the windlass, should he wish to rise to a higher altitude or to come down to the earth again. He now received his final instructions: he was not only to make a written note describing the exact character of the respective positions of the enemy's infantry, artillery, and cavalry, but also to draw a map with materials given him which would show at a glance those positions in their relation to the rest of the surrounding country.

The first perilous moment for our amateur aeronaut was the one at which the balloon would appear above the tops of the trees; being then still near the ground, it would be in range of the hostile guns.

As soon as it should reach a point high up in the sky, the enemy would find it impossible to raise the mouths of their cannon on a line of such sharp elevation as to fire them with any prospect of success.

Two steps were taken that were expected to increase the chance of a safe ascent in the dangerous earliest stage: first, the balloon was placed behind a thicket of pine which would serve as a perfect curtain when the start was made; and secondly, the crew were ordered to let the rope out with great rapidity in the beginning so that the balloon might shoot suddenly far above the intervening screen of trees. The enemy might thus be unable to fire at it before it had risen high in the air.

While their shrapnel might be evaded in the ascent by this precaution, no like means of escaping could be devised for the descent, for, as the balloon came down, its motion earthward was certain to be observed by the hostile cannoneers, who would hold their fire until it was within the range of their guns.

The enemy must have been informed by spies of the intended ascent, for hardly had the balloon risen above the tops of the pines when a cannon in the nearest Federal encampment was hastily elevated and began to discharge shrapnel straight at it. A rain of shells and bullets was scattered about the great floating cotton bag, but fortunately, none of the missiles or their fragments struck either the envelope or the occupant of the basket. Bryan had the presence of mind to wave his flag to the crew below as a signal to them to let the rope run out faster so that a more rapid headway might increase his chance of escaping; a quick response followed; and the balloon shot up so high in a few minutes that the Federal gunners ceased their fire. Bryan again signaled to the crew, and the balloon came to a stop.

The experience through which he had just passed was so exciting that he afterwards acknowledged that, for a time, he was unable to observe the positions of the enemy or to note the probable number of the troops, in the several arms of the service, who might be seen from the great height. Every puff of wind swayed the basket to and fro and caused the enormous bag above him to tug at the rope like some animal trying to escape. Apart from the awful uncertainty of his seat at that fearful altitude, which made his brain dizzy, he could not help thinking of the perils of the descent that he would soon have to face. But gradually his equanimity returned and he was able to perform the task which had brought him into that lofty sphere.

Below him lay the entire region situated between the Chesapeake on the east, James river on the west, and Hampton Roads on the south. It was spread out like a vast map, with all its natural features distinctly visible. A closer inspection revealed the sites of the hostile encampments and the positions of the artillery, infantry, and cavalry. It was no easy job to make a note in writing and draft a map of all that he was able to observe, for the balloon, blown about by the currents in the upper air, soon became as unsteady as if it were a gigantic top spinning slowly in one complete revolution after another.

But after a considerable interval, he was successful in completing in detail the work which he had been ordered to do and signaled to the men on the ground that he was ready to descend. He was now fully aware that he was about to pass through the greatest perils of his entire flight. Nor did he exaggerate them; the enemy clearly understood the value of the information which he would bring General Johnston to aid the Confederate cause and to damage the Federal; and they determined to blow up the balloon and destroy its occupant if it were possible to do so. Instead of one battery being trained on Bryan, as in the ascent, there were now four or five; and so soon as the balloon sank within range of the guns, they opened on it with a violent and continuous fire. The air around it appeared to the lookers-on below to be filled with flame and smoke from the bursting shrapnel.

But again fortune favored Bryan; with such energy did the crew, working in relays, turn the windlass that the balloon descended even more rapidly than it went up; and very soon disappeared from the enemy's sight behind the screen of pine trees. It had made the whole of its dangerous voyage without receiving a single scratch.

General Johnston was very much pleased with his aeronaut's report and warmly praised him for the courage and skill which he had shown. Bryan received these words of commendation with the modesty of a true hero; but he was not eager to put himself in so novel a situation a second time.

"Will you not now, Sir," he asked, "reassign me to my former place with General Magruder?"

"My dear Sir," replied Johnston with his most winning smile, "I fear that you forget that you are the only experienced aeronaut that I have with my army. You will please hold yourself in readiness, as we may wish you to make another ascension at any time."

Within a few days, he received an order to go up in the balloon again. Special precautions were now taken to increase the chances for a safe voyage. A new spot from which the balloon was to be sent up was chosen at some distance from the old. This, it was hoped, would disconcert the enemy's gunners, as they would be looking for its next appearance above the same screen of pines as at first. In addition, a more rapid descent was to be assured by the use of six strong artillery horses hitched to the end of the rope; when the signal should be given by the aeronaut in the sky, these horses were to be ridden at full speed up the road leading right away from the windlass.

The second ascension went off without any mishap, and Bryan now began to think that, after all, General Johnston was right in considering him to be an experienced aeronaut. Anyway, he looked forward to another flight with much less nervousness;

and was not disconcerted when he received the order to go up the third time.

It had been reported by the outposts that the enemy were in motion, and it became of urgent importance to ascertain the exact point on the line of Confederate entrenchments which they were likely to assault first. There was now a full moon and observations could be taken from a point in the sky almost as accurately at night as during the day, and with much less danger. The firing crew were ordered to inflate the balloon at once, and Bryan was directed to enter the basket so soon as the men gave the signal that all was ready. Never had he mounted to his seat with so strong a feeling of confidence, for he now looked on himself as being no longer an amateur. The enemy too would be unable, in spite of the bright moonlight, to follow the ascent of the balloon with as much certainty as during the day; and as they were now advancing, their batteries could not, in their former number at least, hurl shrapnel at their aerial target.

But it is always the unexpected that happens. Bryan almost immediately found himself in a situation encompassed by such dangers as he had never yet been called upon to face. As this balloon was the only one attached to that Confederate army, its ascension was regarded by the soldiers as an event of extraordinary interest; and they always gathered around the fire when the inflation was going on to watch the process, and afterwards to gaze at the great bag as it rose towards the zenith. On this particular occasion, a larger number than usual had assembled, since it was night when most of the men were off duty. The brilliant flames from the pine knot fuel were visible in the half darkness to even the most distant camps, and this drew many additional spectators to the spot; so many, indeed, came to gratify their curiosity that the crew engaged in filling the balloon with hot air found it difficult to perform their task for the pushing, staring crowd about them.

But finally their work was finished. Bryan stepped into the basket; the windlass began to turn; and the balloon rose from the ground. It went up very smoothly until it had reached a height of about two hundred feet, when, with the suddenness of a pistol shot, it fairly darted straight up into the sky as if it had been discharged from some gigantic catapult. The rope had been cut and the balloon was at the mercy of the winds!

The accident had happened in a curious way. It seems that one of the soldiers, in his burning eagerness to watch every stage in the inflation of the balloon, had, without knowing it, stepped in the open centre of the great coil of rope that was to be wound around the windlass as the balloon went up. So soon as the ascent began, this rope started to run out so fast, and with such a disturbing noise, that the man, in his astonishment and confusion, permitted his feet to become entangled, and seeing himself drawn helplessly toward the windlass, screamed at the top of his voice for assistance. A comrade, standing near, thinking that his friend would certainly be caught in the windlass and killed, picked up a hatchet and with a quick blow severed the rope. The man was thus saved from injury or death, but the balloon was set free to rise as high and to float as far as the winds should dictate.

Bryan's sensations, when he found himself darting up to the heavens at the speed of the fastest locomotive, were far more acute and bewildering than they were at the beginning of his first adventure. His breath was taken away; and he could only grip the sides of his basket to save himself from falling out. He afterwards calculated that the balloon only ceased to shoot upwards when it had reached an altitude of two miles: at that height, even had it been during the day, it would have been barely possible for him to discern the exact positions of the enemy, but, at night, although the moon was shining so brightly, all thought of taking observations of what was going on below was wholly impracticable. Even if it had been otherwise, the perils of the aeronaut's situation would not have admitted, in the first stage at least, of his discharging such a duty.

The balloon being now entirely beyond his control, the prospect before him was not a cheerful one; indeed, all the chances were that he would either come to the ground within the enemy's lines or be dropped into Chesapeake Bay. In the one case, he would be imprisoned; in the other, drowned. He knew that the balloon would remain up in the sky as long as the air which it contained should keep its heat. What time must pass before it should begin to cool?

Before the smallest evidence that the heat was diminishing revealed itself, the balloon floated lazily far back behind the Confederate lines. Bryan began to hope that, after all, he was going to escape the capture which he had been foreboding. Then a current of wind struck the sides of the great bag, stopped it, and gradually diverted its motion in the other direction; in a short time, he found himself floating far behind the Federal encampments, and now his heart sank, he was certain that he would be taken prisoner. But again the balloon became the sport of an air current antagonistic to the one propelling it; and under this new pressure, it slowly turned and floated back towards the Confederate entrenchments.

The hot air had now cooled to such a degree that the balloon had sunk to a plane of the atmosphere only a few hundred feet above the ground. But this fact created a new danger. If he passed over the Federal batteries at that height, they would not fail to open fire and bring him to earth; might not the Confederate batteries also send a storm of shrapnel after him in their ignorance as to his identity? He was now so near the surface of the ground that there should be little difficulty in hitting so enormous a target.

Hardly had the balloon arrived over the first Confederate encampment when its occupant was greeted with a fusillade of musketry, and although he frantically waved his signal flag, the soldiers below ran forward some distance, as he receded, firing at the huge object overhead, now clearly visible in the moonlight. Slowly the balloon drifted away until it stood above the margin of York river, and as it passed out over the stream, it had sunk so low that Bryan could distinctly hear the rope that was trailing beneath it splashing in the water.

Fearing that he would be thrown out into the Bay, and that he would be impeded in swimming by a pair of heavy boots which he was wearing, he endeavored to draw them off, but in vain; and it was not until he had ripped their sides wide open with his knife that he at last rid his feet of the obstruction.

While he was fumbling with this task, the balloon, under the influence of another current of air, drifted back to land; and when it had sunk still nearer to the surface of the earth, he grasped the rope, and with the agility of an acrobat, let himself down to the ground by means of it.

Running forward with the end in his hand, he tied it to a tree, and the balloon, already near the last stage of complete collapse, soon settled quietly in a heap on the grass.

CHAPTER FOUR
Lieutenant Robins and the Vanguard

☆　☆　☆　☆

Through the region that lies between the Pamunkey and the James, there flows a river the name of which was on the lips of all men during the spring and summer of 1862; this is the Chickahominy, a stream that, for many miles of its course, is bordered by green swamps and stagnant, pestilential backwaters. In the second year of the war, this marshy stream was crossed by wooden bridges, approached on either side by roadbeds covered over with saplings, laid down one after the other so unevenly as to cause many a jolt to the passing wagon. In this way alone could a firm highway be built on that mass of oozing mud. Back of the swamps, were either narrow low grounds or hills overgrown with stunted trees and scrubby bushes, interspersed with small farms that showed few signs of thrift or prosperity.

It was on the banks of this jungle stream that McClellan posted the great army which he had led up the Peninsula for the capture of the Confederate capital. The position was a dangerous one for that army to occupy should it meet with even a partial defeat, whether on the north or the south side of the river. The Federal success at Fair Oaks, and the coming up of reinforcements, alone prevented the Federal failure at Seven Pines from developing into a disastrous rout.

June had now arrived. The trees were clothed with their

greenest leaves; the fields were carpeted with newly sprung grass; the swamps had become screens of foliage impenetrable to the eye; and the softness and beauty of summer in its earliest flush brooded over the entire landscape. It was in the midst of this scene, so touched by the wand of the loveliest and most promising season of the year, that the two hostile armies stood sternly facing each other, like a couple of gladiators, who, after wrestling together without preponderance for either, have stopped simply to recover their breath. The situation was more disappointing to the Federals, for they were now so near their goal, Richmond, that they could, from the hills, descry the tallest spires of the city and hear the striking of its public clocks.

Lee was soon appointed to take the place of Johnston, who, having been severely wounded, had been compelled to throw up active service. The new commander found his antagonist very firmly entrenched in front of him. A direct attack was not likely to succeed. Would an attack upon the flank?

Lee decided to dispatch a considerable force northward to Hanover Court-House to ascertain the defenses of the Federal right wing, which had been pushed forward to that point in the hope of soon joining hands with McDowell, descending from Washington and Fredericksburg. If the defenses were reported to be weak, Jackson could be brought suddenly and secretly from the Valley to strike the right wing, to double it up, and to throw it back in confusion on the Federal centre; which, simultaneously, might be assaulted directly by the main body of the Confederate troops, now stationed behind their line of breastworks.

The task of getting the information wanted was a dangerous one, and could only be safely entrusted to a very bold yet cautious leader and to picked men and tested horses. There was one officer who possessed, in the highest degree, the daring, the prudence, and the skill required for such an enterprise; this was General J. E. B. Stuart, who commanded all the cavalry belonging to the Confederate army.

The war did not give birth on either side to a more gallant or a more picturesque figure than this famous officer. The spirit of gayety seemed to sit upon the crest of his personality as well in the hour of peril as in the hour of peace; when the first note of the bugle sounding Boots and Saddles was heard, he would leap on his horse with the delighted animation of a man who was about to enter a ballroom for the dance. Riding at the head of his column in the course of a raid that may have taken him far behind the enemy's lines, and even when charging at the head of his men – for he never ordered them to go where he was not ready to go with them – he would burst out into song, indifferent to the clatter of the march or the storm of bursting shells, as if for him the shadow of death had in it something stimulating and exhilarating. His negro banjo player always went along with him in his campaigns to please his master's ear, both on the road and in the tent, with the old plantation melodies.

He was the ideal cavalier in his manner, his stride, and his dress; and in spirit too, for he was equally ready to charge the enemy or to play the gallant to the admiring ladies. "His men," a member of his staff records, "treated him more like the chief huntsman of a hunting party than as a Major-General." His uniform showed his love of gay colors – gold braid and buttons that shone brilliantly adorned his jacket; from his hat, looped up on one side by a golden star, a large plume always floated; his cape, which he usually wore thrown back over his shoulders, was lined with scarlet; his spurs were made of the purest gold; and he not infrequently appeared on the parade and on the march with his horse's neck wreathed in brightly tinted flowers.

Beneath these lighter qualities, there lurked a firmness of courage which no dangers or difficulties could daunt or confuse; a power of endurance which no fatigue could exhaust; and a capacity for military leadership which was relied upon with unquestioning confidence by every officer and private at his back.

Who were the men now detailed to follow this splendid leader upon one of the most dangerous enterprises in which soldiers ever took part? These troopers had been chosen from the body of the Confederate cavalry, perhaps the most accomplished arm of the service, and they had been prepared for the expedition before them by the experience they had recently acquired in Northern Virginia and on the Peninsula. Always the eyes and ears of the army, they had kept up their ceaseless vigil on the enemy's movements throughout the winter and spring, regardless alike of rain and snow and sunshine, and indifferent to the condition of the roads, whether frozen as hard as iron or melted into bottomless mud. The clash of sabres and the rattle of carbines had been ever in their ears; and never were they slow in mounting to the saddle at the first note of the bugle, even should it ring out in the middle of the night. Their only tents had been their blankets, and their only commissary stores such food as they could pick up at the farm-houses along the road.

Indeed, their marches had been full of exciting episodes from day to day and even from hour to hour. Incident and adventure had crowded on them – now they were pursuing or retreating before the enemy; now they were scouting or skirmishing or plunging into a pitched battle. They had drunk deeply of the life of partisans and rangers on a grand scale – at one moment, exposed to all the fatigues of the night raid or to the imminent perils of a clash of arms in the day time; at the next, relaxing under the influence of jovial comradeship in the light of the bivouac fires beneath the boughs of the silent forest – an endless round, as one of their own comrades has written, of marching, fighting, jesting, feasting, starving.

Such had been the recent experiences of the men who were about to set out with Stuart upon what was to prove to be the most brilliant adventure even in his romantic career. There were about fifteen hundred troopers in all. The vanguard, composed of some fifteen picked cavalrymen, was under the command of Lieutenant William T. Robins, an officer even younger in years than Stuart, whom he resembled in his love of fun and frolic, in his buoyant and sanguine disposition, in his fondness for the excitement of battle, and in his perfect contempt for danger. He possessed all the qualities of the typical young Virginian of that period. Before hostilities began, he was a country gentleman distinguished among his fellows for his manly accomplishments – he was a skillful oarsman, a fearless rider, an accurate shot, a graceful dancer, a charming raconteur, a gay and sympathetic companion, and an hospitable host. Having, like Stuart, the keenest relish for a song, he was often heard, as he dashed along in the ride around McClellan's army, trolling "In the Good Old Colony Days," "Bonnie Blue Flag," and other airs which were popular in those stirring times.

When the squadron under Stuart started on the morning of June 12th on their great reconnoisance, not an officer under him, including Lieutenant Robins, who was to lead the vanguard, was aware of the exact destination which the General had in view. Indeed, as we shall see, circumstances were to govern the movements of the expedition. Lieutenant Robins was ordered to keep well in front on the march. He received sixty rounds of ammunition and three day's rations for each soldier under him. This very ignorance as to the real purpose of the enterprise exhilarated his men; they were at least sure that their love of adventure was soon to be fully gratified, probably by a clash with the enemy and certainly by an outing in the open fields and woods. If there was to be any excitement, whether of the attack or the pursuit, they would, as the vanguard, be the first to plunge into it and the first to draw blood. As gaily as if they were about to take part in a fox chase, they leaped upon their horses when the bugle sounded Boots and Saddles; and as they rode away at a fast trot, one of them called out to a small disconsolate group of soldiers left behind in the camp, "Goodbye, boys, we are going to help old Jack drive the Yanks into the Potomac."

So the vanguard conjectured because Lieutenant Robins had received the order to move straight towards the north, which would have brought them in time to Fredericksburg, and in the end into actual conflict with McDowell. Throughout the day, they kept well ahead of the main body, and were untiring in their search for traces of Federal scouts and detachments, who might have stolen that far beyond their lines. The woods were now in their greenest and lushest leaf; the fields were covered with the springing corn or the waving wheat; the weeds had grown tall by the way-side. The vanguard took advantage of all these natural screens, as they wished to be as secret in their movements as the necessity for rapidity should permit.

The first night they went into bivouac with the main forces at a point situated about twenty-two miles north of Richmond; and the next morning, they arose from their couch on the ground without having been aroused by the reveille, as the outposts of the enemy were known to be near at hand and watchful for any sign or sound of a hostile army. The vanguard were now ordered to wheel sharply to the east – which proved to them that they were not expected after all to lead the way towards the Rappahannock. Was it then the General's intention to attack the right wing of McClellan? This wing they knew vaguely was encamped somewhere in the region which they were now facing.

A march of a few miles brought Lieutenant Robins and his men in sight of Hanover Court-House, the drowsy village which Patrick Henry had made famous by his speech against the Parsons, and which contained a quaint old tavern and a few colonial houses shaded by trees that had been standing there in the times of the Revolution. In its single street, they saw a large detachment of Federal horses tied to the fences, but all saddled so that they could be mounted at the first alarm. Robins immediately reported this fact to General Stuart, who moved forward in front, while Colonel Fitzhugh Lee was ordered to attack on the flank; but before either could come in range of the enemy, a party of cavalry scouts, they had retreated in a cloud of dust eastward down the road leading to Old Church.

The vanguard took up the pursuit at top speed, and at a heavily wooded spot known as Hawes Shop they ran pell mell upon the Federal pickets, whom they either captured or dispersed. Not halting one minute, they continued their headlong gallop until they came suddenly in sight of a large body of Federal troopers blocking the highway with sabres drawn for a charge. These troopers had their camp at Old Church, and having been alarmed by the retreating scouts, whom their commander had sent to Hanover Court-House to reconnoitre, they had advanced to ascertain the strength of the raiding party. They were too formidable a force for the vanguard to attack alone, so they drew off until Colonel W. H. F. Lee should reach the ground at the head of his squadrons.

From this point the road ran through a deep ravine down to the banks of Tottopotomoi Creek, which it crossed by a wooden bridge. The steep sides of the highway were fringed with a thick growth of pine and laurel.

On coming up, the large Confederate force now called into action received the order, "Form fours, draw sabre, charge." The Federals resisted only for a short time, as they were outnumbered, and then wheeling in their tracks, retired at a gallop towards the creek, with the Confederates in hot pursuit; but as the road grew more narrow and the woods on either side more dense, Stuart sounded a halt for fear of an overwhelming attack from ambush. The mud-banks of the Tottopotomoi, overgrown with tall weeds and scrubby trees, were now in sight. The bridge was found to be undefended, and Robins was directed to cross with his vanguard and to ascertain whether the enemy had made a stand further on. Having passed over a hill, he discovered a large Federal force drawn up at a point where they would be in position to obstruct the Confederates' advance towards Mechanicsville, in which neighborhood a part of McClellan's army was encamped.

The vanguard again halted for support to march up. Colonel W. H. F. Lee was soon on the ground, and having arranged his troopers in columns of four, as in the first brush, and with sabres drawn, he ordered the advance. As the men galloped forward, yelling at the top of their voices, the Federal skirmishers, hidden in the bushes on either side of the way, became panic stricken, and rushed out into the road at a point where there was an unoccupied interval between the charging Confederate squadron behind and the vanguard under Robins in front. They fled down the highway towards the main body of the Federal cavalry, carrying Robins and his men with them as in an irresistible torrent. In the general melèe that resulted, this little band found themselves shot at with pistols and slashed with sabres by the skirmishers at their back and the

Federal cavalry in their face; and at the end of a brief time, all except their leader were wounded and disabled. Robins finally succeeded in escaping in the confusion by leaping his horse over the fence that bounded the road; and having made a short circuit through the woods, joined the main body of the Confederate pursuers.

Colonel Fitzhugh Lee now came up to continue the attack, which had met with a strong resistance; but in the end, the Federals retreated to Old Church; and on the Confederates arriving there, withdrew in the direction of McClellan's main encampments on the Chickahominy.

When General Lee had sent Stuart to ascertain the defences of the Federal right wing, he had ordered him to march as far as Old Church, and having reached that place, to be guided in his subsequent movements by circumstances. Stuart had now gathered up all the information that the Confederate Commander was seeking – he had learned that the Federal right wing had not been spread out in force as far as Hanover Court-House; and that it was so unprotected on this side that Jackson, coming down from the Valley, could be safely left to attack it with a view of driving it back, to the confusion of the Federal centre; which then might be assaulted by Lee in front with every prospect of success.

Should Stuart return by the route by which he had come, which would take him around again in front of McClellan's army, or should he sweep behind that army, and passing over the Chickahominy river by one of the lower fords, join Lee at a point south of Richmond?

It was a momentous question, and in his decision, Stuart was not influenced entirely by love of spectacular adventure. He could not cross the Pamunkey, now in his neighborhood, and circle about south of Fredericksburg, because he had no pontoons with which to bridge this broad deep stream. If he attempted to retreat to the north of Hanover Court-House, he would run upon the North Anna, now overflowing its banks from recent rains. If he endeavored to pass as before through Hanover Court-House, he would have to defy a concentrated force of Federal artillery, cavalry, and infantry, since the alarm had been given of his presence behind the Federal lines. Could he avoid interception? He thought not.

On the other hand, the prospect of a ride to the lower Chickahominy was not an assuring one, for he would have to advance all the way in sight of the smoke from McClellan's camp fires. Moreover, he was aware that he would have to cross the Richmond and York River Railway, the Federal main line of communication, by which many thousand troops could, within a few hours, be brought down to throw themselves athwart his path. It all depended upon whether the Federal Commander had been promptly informed of his arrival at Old Church. Could there be much room for doubt on that vital point?

In reality, there was barely one chance in ten that he would be able, by rapid movement, to reach the railway before the Federal troops could be concentrated; but this chance he determined to take as offering the safer course among the alternatives open to him. Besides, General Lee had instructed him to inflict all the damage he could on the enemy's communications with West Point, and for the first time during the expedition, he would have an excellent opportunity of doing this so soon as he came up to the railroad.

He was further confirmed in his decision by the fact that he was accompanied by several scouts who were familiar with the country to be traversed; above all, the leader of his vanguard, Lieutenant Robins, having been born in the adjacent county, had known the entire region from boyhood.

Now began the most adventurous stage in the whole course of the ride, and the troopers entered upon it in a spirit of unrestrained gayety. They paused at Old Church just long enough to burn all the tents of the Federal camp and to stuff their haversacks with food from the enemy's stores. As they moved along, the country people flocked to the roadside, and filled their outstretched hands with all sorts of dainties. To Stuart, they gave a bouquet of beautiful flowers, and begged him to carry it back to Richmond with him; which he smilingly promised to do.

In conversation with his officers, he told them that he intended to cut his way through, should he be opposed by either infantry or cavalry; and as his squadrons were now behind the Federal lines, and with reason too to think that their advance was known to McClellan, they held themselves in readiness to charge on the instant. Their sabres were kept drawn and their carbines unslung. At one place, the cry arose, "The Yankees are in the rear." At once, the sabres flashed, fours were formed, and the men at command wheeled about; but not an enemy was to be seen. A roar of laughter swelled from the ranks, and they went on their way in an even gayer mood than before.

All along the road, they passed wagons that had been overturned and deserted and their loads scattered on the ground; but they had no time to halt and pick up the articles they saw. In one spot, the mud was so deep in the roadbed that the two pieces of artillery accompanying them got firmly stalled. At first, it was found impossible to draw out one of the guns; the horses attached to it were lashed, the drivers swore, but the wheels could not be made to budge.

"Why don't you pull that gun out of the mud?" cried the officer in charge, in his impatience.

"Can't be done, Sir," was the discouraged reply.

"Put that keg of whiskey on the caisson," ordered the officer, pointing to a keg in sight. "You men can have it if you drag the gun out."

The keg was placed on the caisson; the cannoneers seized the wheels of the gun carriage; and though it was loaded down with ammunition as well as with the heavy gun barrel itself, they lifted it up and placed it on dry ground; and then the contents of the keg were generously distributed by the winners among all who thirsted for a draft.

Lieutenant Robins and his men were again acting as the vanguard, which consisted now of thirty men, who kept always half a mile ahead of the main column. Their first objective was the country road running from West Point to Richmond, a highway of great military importance, as it was skirted by a line of telegraph wire, which was now in the use of the Federal army on the Chickahominy. Robins had been ordered to cut this wire; and hardly had he done so, when a Federal wagon loaded with revolvers was overtaken by the men and captured. While they were leisurely making their choice of these fine weapons, a small body of Federal troopers came in sight, but immediately halted when they discovered the presence of the Confederate cavalry-men. Drawing their sabres, they arranged their ranks for a charge; but as their opponents had mounted at once and offered a resolute front, and there was a chance too that other Confederate soldiers were close at hand, the Federal officer hesitated to sound the advance. Both of the bands stood with their carbines and sabres prepared for immediate action, and yet each was reluctant to take the first step, in their apprehension of a superior force behind. The Federal commander was wise in showing such prudence, for within the space of a few minutes a Confederate squadron approached at a gallop, and the Federal troopers, outnumbered, quickly retreated down the road.

But not before one of them had been dispatched to Tunstall's station on the railway nearby to warn the guards at that place of the advance of the Confederate cavalrymen. The man was so alarmed that, instead of stopping at the station in obedience to his orders, he passed by it at the top of his horse's speed, making for the protection of the gunboats at the White House on the Pamunkey. As he rushed by, one of the company detailed to defend the station called out to him, "What's to pay?"

"Hell's to pay," was the reply, as the trooper disappeared behind a bend in the highway.

Lieutenant Robins, at the head of his squad of gay and adventurous cavalrymen, continued to lead the way. They were now only five miles distant from McClellan's nearest encampment, and if information had already reached him of the raid, his first step naturally would have been to transport a large body of troops by rail to Turnstall's to head off and destroy the Confederate force. But Stuart was not harassed by the thought of such interception; he was really debating in his own mind whether he should not march straight for the White House and burn the immense accumulation of military stores there, after driving off the six hundred men in charge of them and defying the gunboats in the river.

He wisely decided that it would be too hazardous for him to undertake such a venture in the short time at his disposal. Robins was ordered to push on to Turnstall's, while the squadrons were to follow rapidly in his track. As soon as the vanguard sighted the station, they were drawn up in ranks of four, and at the word of command, charged down on it, with yells that rang through the forests. No resistance was encountered; indeed, the Federal soldiers were lounging about the place without the slightest expectation of an attack. Only one man escaped capture; he had rushed for his musket, but desisted when a Confederate trooper waved his sabre over his head and sternly ordered him to surrender; which he did; but afterwards got away by gliding under the bridge in the confusion and dashing away to the woods.

When all the Federals had been secured, the vanguard busied themselves with felling a big tree across the rails in the hope of stopping any train which might be passing the station. While they were so employed, the main body arrived on the ground, and all were about to lend a hand to place additional obstructions, when the rumbling of an approaching train was heard; the order was quickly given to level their muskets, but the engineer, instead of being intimidated by the sight of the tree lying across the track, and of a whole squadron of men ready to fire, turned the steam on at full head, and swept by at his highest rate of speed. A fusillade greeted the huddled-up Federal soldiers aboard, killing and wounding a large number of them; but the prostrate tree was knocked clear of the rails and the train rushed beyond the bridge and disappeared.

The Confederates now directed their attention to burning this structure, in which they had been interrupted, and to sending up in flames the freight cars standing at the station and numerous wagons parked in a nearby field, all loaded with different kinds of supplies for the Federal army. The telegraph line was cut and the rails torn up for some distance. The whole day was spent in carrying out this destruction.

The troopers were now very much fatigued. They had not rested since they left Old Church; and their only food had been obtained from the country people. The horses too were very much exhausted; the advance had been so rapid that they had been unable to crop by the wayside; and as there had been no halt, they had never been turned into the pastures to forage. But the position of the raiding squadrons was now too precarious to permit of their remaining any longer where they were; it might even turn out that they had already delayed their departure too many hours; Boots and Saddles was sounded; and the troopers fell in promptly on the jaded horses.

Lieutenant Robins again received the order to lead the vanguard. This body was directed to ride some distance ahead of the main column and to await its arrival at the little village of New Baltimore, several miles south of Tunstall's and on the main road running to the ford in the Chickahominy by which Stuart proposed to cross the river. On reaching this village, Lieutenant Robins and his men found there a store which had been erected by a camp follower of McClellan's army with the view of profiting by the trade of the numerous soldiers passing between the encampments near Richmond and the White House on the Pamunkey. This store was stocked with such an assortment of delicacies as to make the hungry Confederates feel as if a full grocery had been suddenly thrown open to them; there were figs, pickles, lemons, preserves, cakes, biscuits, sausages, canned meats, and other articles of food equally satisfying to a starved appetite. Little was left of the original contents of the store when the squadrons behind drew rein in the hamlet.

At Talleysville, a halt was made to allow the main body three hours of rest. They learned here from scouts that there was an interval of only four miles between them and a large force in pursuit; and the latter would have caught up had they continued their march after darkness fell; but this they considered it too dangerous for them to do; and Stuart, setting out for the Chickahominy at midnight had, by the morning, left them well in the rear.

Lieutenant Robins and his band still led the way. There was now a full moon shining and its rays lighted up the road as they trotted along. It was quite possible for the enemy to have already pushed a large force across the path to the Chickahominy which they were now pursuing; and, therefore, it was not an unprovoked imagination on their part that caused them to see in every ghostly bush a blue-coated sentinel; and in every jagged tree a lonely vidette.

Day was just streaking the eastern sky when the vanguard halted at the ford. To their acute disappointment, they found the waters of the stream in flood, and there did not seem to them to be any prospect of the squadron effecting a crossing at that point. They waited for Colonel W. H. F. Lee to come up, as his regiment was the one in front. On his arrival, the question arose: Should they attempt to swim the river in spite of the high water? As the line of crossing from bank to bank was somewhat up stream, the horses would be brought directly against the rushing current so soon as they started for the other side. In the face of this obvious peril, Colonel Lee spurred his horse into the flood; but after getting over with the utmost difficulty, returned to pronounce the passage impracticable for the main body; and especially for the two pieces of artillery. Notwithstanding this conclusion, some seventy-five horsemen succeeded in reaching the farther shore.

In vain, an attempt was made to bridge the river by felling large trees which grew on the bank; the terrific current carried them away so soon as they fell into the water.

"What do you think of the situation. Colonel Lee?" said a member of Stuart's personal staff, who had ridden up.

"Well, Captain," he replied, "I think we are caught."

Stuart, who was now on the ground, refused to admit that he was entrapped. Learning that there was a bridge about a mile down stream, he set his whole force in motion; but on arriving there, found that the wooden part of the structure had been carried away by floods, and that only the stone abutments remained. There was a distance of forty feet between them, and in this narrow bed the stream rushed along as in a mill race. A boat was found tied to the bank, and by means of a rope it was placed and kept in the centre of this speeding water. Planks were let down to the boat from either abutment until a footbridge was constructed from pier to pier, resting on the boat as the middle pier.

Removing the saddles, the troopers swam the horses across, while they themselves passed over this improvised structure. But how was the artillery to be got to the other side? The bridge was not strong enough to sustain the weight of the two field pieces. Stuart ordered his men to bring the beams from an old barn standing in an adjacent field and to adjust their ends to either abutment, and then to cover these supports with planks resting crosswise. While this work was being done, he was not content to look on, but at every stage, gave his personal aid, singing as he did so as gayly as if there was not the smallest danger of a large Federal force coming up at any moment and attacking his rear.

The artillery having been brought over, the whole body of cavalry was soon again in motion. They now found themselves on an island. There was no bridge over the second arm of the river, but men and cannon were able to pass the ford without difficulty or delay. The road between the two branches of the stream, and beyond, was full of mud, and the mules, on which the prisoners were riding, were constantly stumbling, and many of them rolled over in the mud holes. This made it very uncomfortable for the captives, and at last, one of them exclaimed, "How many Chickenhominies are there in this confounded country?"

In the course of the bridge building, Lieutenant Robins and his squad had been acting as the rear guard. From a hill on the north bank of the river, they had been keeping a close watch for the expected approach of the enemy. So soon as the artillery and the main body had crossed, the rear guard drew back to the stream, and when they had passed over, they set the bridge on fire by means of a large quantity of dry fence rails which they had piled up on the planks. They had first tied their horses behind a thick screen of trees, but while the bridge was burning, they themselves, with their leader, stood or were seated in the open road. Hardly had the timbers fallen in, when a shot rang through the swamp, and a small twig, cut by a bullet from the tree overhead, fell into the lap of Lieutenant Robins, who was seated under its boughs.

The shot had come from a soldier belonging to a detachment of Federal Lancers which was in pursuit; the bridge being down, they could not advance any further; and they soon turned back to rejoin their main army.

As the post of danger in the beginning of the ride had been in front, so now it was in the rear; and until Stuart came to James river, this post was filled by Lieutenant Robins and his men. Crossing the second arm of the Chickahominy, they had hurried forward until they had found themselves once more in touch with the main body. Of the thirty-five miles which had now to be traversed before Richmond could be reached, about twenty lay within the lines of the enemy. For thirty-six hours all the men had been almost continuously in the saddle, with few opportunities to refresh themselves with sleep or food. Not far from James river, they halted for a short time to turn their horses out to graze in a clover field, while they devoured the rations picked up by their foragers among the farmhouses. In spite of their fatigue, all felt in a state of elation over the successful course of the raid; many a humorous anecdote was told, and many a joke was cracked by the wags among the troopers.

So soon as night came on, the march was resumed. Once more Lieutenant Robins and his men formed the vanguard. Although their members had so lately rested, yet there were few among them who were not overcome with drowsiness; some, indeed, were so overwhelmed by sleep that they almost fell from their saddles. The road they were marching along was close to James river, which, in this part of it, was occupied by a fleet of Federal war vessels. The moon was now riding high in the sky, and its light, shining on the surface of the water, disclosed the presence of the gunboats. They had but a few minutes before noted a large number of masts, when the challenge rang out: "Who goes there?"

The men were wide awake in an instant; sabres were drawn; and ranks of four formed to repel an attack; but it was quickly found out that a Confederate and not a Federal vidette had raised the cry.

Once more, the vanguard was safe within the Confederate lines; and they were soon followed by the main force.

In the course of this romantic raid by Stuart's squadrons, only one Confederate soldier lost his life; not one of his men was taken prisoner; and only a few were wounded. They brought out one hundred and sixty-five captives, two hundred and sixty horses and mules, and a considerable quantity of small arms. Above all, they secured the information that McClellan's left wing was open to assault; and that Jackson could safely launch his troops against it with the view of throwing it into confusion and pushing it back upon the centre of the Federal army. The ability of fifteen hundred men to ride completely around one hundred and thirty-four thousand, not massed but strung out in a long line, and to ride too within five miles of their principal encampments, had the effect of shaking the confidence of the North in the vigilance and promptitude of the Federal Commander, and this was doubtless one of the influences that led him, later on, to retreat to the protection of his gunboats anchored in James river.

CHAPTER FIVE
The Marion of the West

☆   ☆   ☆   ☆

General John H. Morgan was perhaps the most romantic of all the conspicuous figures associated with the Confederate armies beyond the Alleghanies. No other officer of those armies was the hero of more amazing adventures or evinced more dauntless courage or more perfect self-possession in hazardous situations; he was at once the Western Mosby and the Western Stuart, the daring partisan and the dashing cavalry leader; or as his admiring comrades liked to characterize him, the Marion of the West, whose exploits rivaled those of the famous "Swamp Fox" of the Revolution.

The numerous tales of bravery which are recorded of him illustrate at once his complete imperturbability in the most perilous circumstances, and his astounding resourcefulness in escaping unharmed from them.

During the early occupation of Nashville by the Federals under General McCook, it occurred to Morgan, at that time simply a captain, that he might, by a ruse, decoy a large body of Federal troops into an ambush. Disguising himself as a rough farmer, and accompanied by one of his comrades, who assumed the like part, he drove a wagon to the city loaded down with bags of meal which he had bought of a country miller. Having found out beforehand the name of the hotel where General McCook ate his meals, he stopped his wagon in front of it, and entered as if for the purpose of getting dinner, but really for the purpose of talking with the Federal Commander if he should happen to have come in. Fortunately, the General in uniform was already seated at one of the tables, and Morgan perceived who he was at a glance.

"Is this heah Gineral McCook," said he, when he had, with exaggerated clumsiness, shambled into the chair at his side.

"That's my name," replied the General cordially.

"Wall, Gineral," said Morgan, in slow and drawling tones, "if thar's no Secesh 'bout, I've got sum'pen ter tell you right heah. I live up close by Burk's Mills in the middle of a nest of red hot Seceshers and they swar' yer sojers shant hev a speck o' meal if they starve for it. But, Gineral, I got a wagon load of meal ground, and I hev' brung it down heah ter day, and it's now out thar in the street and you kin hev it if yer want it."

General McCook, pleased by the loyal and helpful spirit of the farmer, thanked him warmly for his generosity, and then graciously added, "Take the meal, my friend, to the Commissary. He will pay you for it in gold and silver."

Morgan quietly finished his dinner; then rising from his seat as clumsily as he had sat down, bowed awkwardly to the General and shambled out of the room.

After a half hour, he entered the Federal Headquarters, where, he was told, General McCook would then be found.

"Gineral," he said, "can't yer send one hundred and fifty men up thar to the neberhood of Burk's Mills? I'll guide 'em into that nest er traitors and seceshers; and they kin capture too a mighty big sight er meal."

Again General McCook thanked him very heartily for his patriotic zeal.

"The men, my friend," he said emphatically, "shall certainly be sent. What day shall we choose? Let the appointment be as early as possible. I suppose this is a busy time with you farmers, but when one's country calls, the plough itself must stop in the furrow."

After stoutly asserting his willingness to let everything go to ruin from neglect rather than lose the chance of seizing those "seceshers," the loyal farmer named the day and hour for the rendezvous. When the Federal soldiers reached the spot thus agreed upon, they were confronted by Captain Morgan at the head of so many Confederate troopers that they surrendered without firing a shot.

On another occasion, Morgan was returning on horseback from a raid alone when he saw ahead of him, in front of a house by the roadside, a Federal officer; and he inferred from sounds overheard by him that there were several soldiers inside the building. He suspected that these men belonged to the Federal picket line, and that, without permission, they had left their posts. Being dressed in the full uniform of a higher Federal officer himself, he boldly rode up to the real Federal officer and peremptorily charged him and his comrades with deliberate neglect of duty.

"Give me your pistol," he sternly commanded.

The officer reluctantly complied.

"Now order the men in the house to come out one by one and deliver up their arms. I shall go with you to headquarters and report you for abandoning your post."

Just as the last soldier handed over his pistol and carbine, a member of Morgan's band came up with four prisoners; six were then added to that number; and the ten were marched to a camp within the Confederate lines.

Another story is told of Morgan and a telegraph operator at Lebanon, Kentucky, who was employed by the Federals, for, at the time of the incident, that town was in their possession. The operator had just forwarded to Nashville a telegram received from Louisville ordering the transfer to the latter city of all the prisoners of Morgan's command recently captured, as, at any hour, the Confederate partisan might make a dash for Nashville and carry them off. This suggestion caused the operator to feel very uncomfortable, as he afterwards related.

"Who knows," he exclaimed to himself, "but that guerrilla may pounce like a hawk on me too. If I only had him here, wouldn't I put an end to his villainy!"

Hearing the sound of a horse's hoofs on the road outside, he went to the window to find out who the rider was. A man dressed in a butternut suit and wearing a shabby slouched hat had just dismounted and was tying his horse to a fence near the door. He soon entered the house.

"What's the news?" he asked in drawling accents that seemingly revealed little interest in his own question.

"No news," was the curt reply of the operator, who, with a yawn, sat down again at his instrument.

The stranger leisurely picked up a copy of the Louisville *Journal* which lay on a desk at his right hand.

"John Morgan is raiding again, I see," he remarked as if speaking to himself. "What a pity that man cannot be caught!"

The words seemed to strike a passionate chord in the operator's breast, for he jumped up from his seat, and walking backwards and forwards across the room in a state of vindictive rage, almost shouted out, "Yes, the scoundrel, the villain! If I only had him here, I'd blow his brains out this very moment! Just let him enter that door and he is a dead man!"

The operator made a furious gesture, as if he were burning, not only to kill the partisan chief, but also to mangle and mutilate his body beyond all chance of recognition.

The stranger quietly replaced the paper on the top of the desk; then rose from his seat, and stopping in front of the operator – who, fuming and sputtering, was still striding up and down the room like a lunatic shut up in a cage – said to him in his gentlest voice, as he held out towards him a pistol which he had taken from his hip pocket, "I am John Morgan. Now execute your threat."

The operator stared at him aghast, and then in a state almost of collapse from sheer fright at the sound of that dreaded name, stammered out, "I, I – didn't know – I hadn't any idea – that you were Colonel Morgan, Sir – indeed, Sir, I didn't – I beg pardon, Sir, ten thousand times, Sir."

The man as he spoke kept backing away, with his hands held out in the most deprecating manner, until he found himself squarely against the wall. His face was as pallid and his voice as tremulous as if he expected to be shot at once.

"Be quick," said Morgan, looking at him sternly and contemptuously, "I have a message for Louisville to dictate. If you falsify it, your life will be the forfeit."

The operator hastened to reseat himself at the instrument, a picture of crestfallen submissiveness; nor were his apprehensions lessened by the thought of the cocked pistol which Morgan held to his head while repeating, word by word, the misleading message which he wished to be forwarded. When it had been dispatched, with a promptness never before surpassed in that office, he said, "Now, let me have at once all the telegrams that you have sent or received during the last twenty-four hours."

The operator hastily gathered them together and obsequiously placed them in Morgan's hands; who read them with close attention. Having given the operator a few stern words of warning to hold his tongue in the future, Morgan left the room, mounted his horse, and quietly rode away.

One of the most audacious incidents recorded of Morgan is the following. Accompanied by a Confederate officer, both disguised by Federal uniforms, he was making, with a dozen prisoners, for the protection of the Confederate lines. Suddenly he found himself facing a body of two thousand blue-coats.

"Halt," cried their commander, as he rode forward, "give the countersign."

"Countersign!" exclaimed Morgan, assuming an air of indignation, "what do you mean by demanding the countersign of an officer of my rank? Order your companies to fall apart so as to give room for the passage of my men."

The Federal prisoners with Morgan, instead of informing on him at once, silently entered into the spirit of his critical situation, as they were curious to see how far his ingenuity could assist him to escape. They did not look upon this conduct as treasonable because they were sure they could stop him should there be any prospect of his really getting away. Just as if they were acting as his escort, they followed him and his Confederate comrade, without a word, between the two long files of Federal soldiers, and were careful to suppress all signs of their amusement over the deceptive part which they themselves were playing for the moment. At one point in the path of the little cavalcade, several of the Federal officers stood so far out as to block their progress. "Move up," cried Morgan impatiently, "you are no better than deserters. Morgan will catch you yet."

So soon as he and his fellow Confederate reached the last soldier in their passage between the files, they turned and waved their hands to the prisoners; and before they could be either stopped or fired upon, leaped a fence and vanished in a body of thick woods that grew close at hand.

In his numerous raids, Morgan was always accompanied by a skillful telegraph operator, who carried his instrument behind his saddle. On one occasion, it was very important for him to find out whether there were any Federal troops at Louisville who could be transported in a hurry to Bowling Green to reinforce the large body stationed there, should this become necessary as the only means of intercepting him and his men while scouring the country behind the Federal lines. General Boyle was in command at Louisville, and General Granger at Bowling Green. Morgan advanced without interference to a station situated on the main railway joining the two cities. His operator was there ordered to attach his instrument to the wires and to put himself in direct communication with General Boyle; Boyle was then informed, in a message sent in the name of General Granger, that Morgan had been seen in the neighborhood of Bowling Green; and that there was immediate danger of his attacking that town. How many troops could Boyle dispatch at the end of the next few hours to reinforce Granger?

"There are no troops in Louisville who can be made at once available," was the prompt reply.

"Are there troops elsewhere who could be sent to Bowling Green? If so, where are they now? How soon could they be brought up to strengthen that town's defenses?"

Boyle, in his answer to this second telegram, named the places where troops were then stationed; stated their exact number; and calculated the time within which they could be transported to Bowling Green.

Having received this explicit and comprehensive reply, Morgan sent off his final telegram, in which he thanked General Boyle for giving him so much valuable information and praised him as "a very smart boy." This message was signed by him with his own name.

CHAPTER SIX
Morgan Crosses the Ohio

☆　☆　☆　☆

The boldest of General Morgan's exploits was his raid beyond the Ohio river in 1863. During that year, he was directed by General Bragg, who was hard pressed by General Rosecranz, to set out with a considerable body of troops towards Louisville, as a threatened attack on that city would be sure to create a diversion in favor of the Confederate army, now falling back through Tennessee. Colonel Basil Duke, a soldier as intrepid and as enterprising in spirit as Morgan himself, was chosen to be the second in command. As the men started northward, they sang in concert:

> Here's a health to Duke and Morgan
> Drink it down.
> Here's a health to Duke and Morgan.
> Down, boys, down, drink it down.

Breaking through the fierce opposition at the crossing of the Cumberland and defying the Federal cavalrymen gathering in his rear, Morgan advanced rapidly towards the Ohio river. On the fourth of July, he encountered several companies of Michigan troopers.

"Surrender" was the laconic and peremptory message which he sent to the Federal commander.

"I shall not lower my flag on Independence Day," was the stout reply.

In the battle which at once followed, Morgan lost one hundred men either killed or wounded, and was forced to make a wide detour in order to shake off the clutch of his gallant foe. In the next skirmish, his brother, who was still a mere boy, the favorite of all his comrades and rash and brave to the last fibre, was left a corpse on the field, to the poignant grief of the whole command.

Would Morgan halt on the bank of the Ohio at a point about forty miles west of Louisville, for which he was making, or would he cross it, with the intention of pushing his raid into the States of Indiana and Ohio, and at the end coming back into Kentucky by fording the river east of Cincinnati? This was a perilous enterprise which had only a bare chance of success; but for this very reason, it appealed all the more irresistibly to the intrepid partisan who now decided to undertake it.

As he drew near to the Ohio, he sent a company ahead to capture two steamers which were lying in the stream at the point where he had planned to cross; and on his own arrival there, he found these boats with steam up and ready to carry his men over. There was such a heavy fog prevailing that the other shore was entirely hidden from view; but fearing lest the Federal cavalry in pursuit of him should appear at any minute, he marched his troops on board in spite of the mist. Before the ropes, however, could be cast off, there came the roar of a cannon and the rattle of musketry from the Indiana side. The fog now lifted and a few shots from one of his Parrott guns caused the Federal militia, which had done the firing, to skurry away to a wooded hill in the rear.

The transfer of Morgan's troopers now began, and when one half had succeeded in crossing, a small steamboat paddled suddenly in sight and started to shell the two Confederate detachments, now separated by the stream. The situation for Morgan's men became highly critical – one section was waiting on one shore for the other section, which was now held to the opposite shore. At any moment, the Federal cavalry in pursuit might come up on the Kentucky side; while the militia posted on the hill back of the

Indiana bank might already have been reinforced. The two wings could thus be easily crushed without being able to afford each other any assistance; but after a sharp duel with the Parrott guns, the steamboat drew off, and the Confederates on the Kentucky bank took advantage of its retreat to join their comrades, anxiously expecting them on the Indiana side.

Once more the march was taken up. The vanguard as they advanced again sang:

> Here's a health to Duke and Morgan,
> Drink it down.

And the rear guard replied in tones that could be heard by the men in front in spite of the distance:

> The race is not to them that's got
> The longest legs to run,
> Nor the battle to that people
> That shoots the biggest gun.

As Morgan's veterans plunged deeper into the country, they ran up against large bodies of militia barricaded behind the rail fences; but being untrained, they were easily dispersed. The people scattered at the Confederates' approach as a flock of chickens scatters at the shadow of a hawk. Their larders were found wide open, and their abandoned kitchen stoves were covered with cooked or half baked meats and vegetables, which the hungry invaders did not scruple to take and devour. Only one house was set on fire, and this was thus treated because it had been used as an improvised fortress. Everywhere the wires were cut to prevent the transmission of news of the Confederate advance, which would have led at once to a concentration of hostile troops to block all farther progress.

There was stationed at Cincinnati a large body of Federal soldiers, and as Morgan drew near to this city, he was aware that the chances of his interception had been increased by its proximity; but this did not cause him to hesitate to continue his march straight for that place. He was hopeful that he had confused the reports as to his movements by his mystifying telegrams; and that the greater number of the Federal troops originally concentrated there, had, in consequence, been broken up into widely dispersed detachments, which were searching for him in the wrong directions. His own force was very much reduced by deaths, wounds, and captures; but he was confident that he could beat off whatever small body of men might still be on guard in Cincinnati, should they leave their post there and venture outside. He concluded not to enter its streets even if no opposition was met with as he approached the suburbs, for he anticipated that each house would be made a small fortress; and that his soldiers, ignorant of the town, would become too widely separated to be called together again in their original number.

In passing around the northern suburbs of Cincinnati, the men were perplexed by the intricacies of the roads; and they also found it difficult to keep in touch with each other, as the track of the first column of troopers was frequently blotted out by the clouds of dust that followed them, so that the second column were often compelled, in the general darkness, to guess at the way which, their comrades had taken. All were now so exhausted by hard travel that many, in their drowsiness, slipped from their horses to the ground, and when they had picked themselves up, stumbled under the cover of the shrubbery, and throwing themselves down, went fast to sleep.

Although most of the horses were sprung from the thoroughbred stock of Kentucky, yet few of them remained fresh after their journey of a thousand miles. Many that started off with the raid had long since given out and been exchanged by their owners for common horses belonging to farmers in Indiana and Ohio; but so great was the affection felt for the abandoned steeds, that, in parting with them, the troopers were seen to shed tears of poignant regret.

Morgan had now pushed far to the east of Cincinnati; and at Williamsburg, he decided to halt men and horses for the night in order that they might obtain the rest which they so much need-

The column was turned towards Buffington Island.

ed. The spirits of the soldiers were greatly refreshed by a long and deep sleep; and next morning they awoke in as gay a temper as when they rode out of Tennessee towards the North. There were two violins, a banjo, and a guitar in the camp and several white and black musicians. The columns were now close to the bank of the Ohio, and across its waters they could see the green hills of Kentucky. The chords of "Old Kentucky Home" were struck on the several instruments, and the strain was taken up by the voices of group after group until it echoed far over the water.

Breaking camp, the head of the column was turned straight towards Buffington Island, where it was Morgan's intention to cross the river by a ford which was in use at that point. Scouts sent ahead returned and reported that the direct road to this ford was blocked by a force of three hundred Federal infantrymen, who had thrown up formidable breastworks. Federal cavalrymen were already in swift pursuit of the retiring Confederates, and it looked as if they would be caught between the two detachments of the enemy and either killed or captured. Hurrying forward, several hundred troopers were able, by a short detour, under the cover of fog, to reach the head of the ford in safety and to cross to the southern side. The remainder found themselves practically surrounded; Federal forces assaulted them from behind and in front at the same moment; and to make their position more hopeless, several gunboats, which had come up the river, poured a heavy fire into their unprotected ranks. The few who were not captured or killed escaped by dispersing in small bodies and working away from the river.

Morgan had succeeded in reaching the middle of the river safely, when, seeing the plight of his men on the Ohio bank, he turned his horse's head and swam back to share their fate. As he came ashore, the negro banjo player, whose name was Box, plunged into the water to escape to the Kentucky side.

"Come back," shouted the General to him. "You will certainly drown."

"No, Marse John," cried Box, "if dey ketch you, dey prole (parole) you, but if dey ketch dis nigger in a Free State, he ain't gwine to git away while dis war lasts."

The boy succeeded in swimming without mishap the long distance across the river and returned unhurt to his Kentucky home, there to stuff his family with marvelous tales of his part in the great raid, and to soothe his own war-worn spirit by daily repetition of the plantation melodies which he had played on that famous march.

During six days, Morgan was able to elude his pursuers; but at the end of that time, had to give himself up, together with two hundred brave comrades who had followed him to the last ditch. With half a dozen of these faithful men, he was shut up in the cells of the Ohio State Prison. The constant movement in the open air which had marked their lives during the raid, so disastrously terminated, made their confinement within four dark bare walls, in a very close atmosphere, almost intolerable to them, and they resolved, if possible, to effect their escape from the toils.

But how was this to be brought about? Fortunately for them, they had access to each other from cell to cell during the night and day alike, which enabled them to act in concert in carrying out the plan that they finally agreed on. The only practicable way of getting out was by forcing an entrance to the basement; and to accomplish this, they were compelled to bore through a cement floor, which was almost as hard as if it had been laid in granite. Several men were soon engaged in the work of excavation under the cover of the bed in one of the cells; others were employed in making ropes by tearing the sheets and ticking into strips and twisting them stoutly together; while still others were converting everything about their quarters that was at all suitable for the purpose into uncouth weapons for self-defense and attack.

During the time the prisoners were so occupied, they had to show the most unvarying prudence, for the sentinel was likely to appear amongst them at any moment of the day or night. At night, he regularly visited the doors of the cells once every three hours and thrust his lantern between the bars to find out whether the men were all there and asleep; and not content with this, would often return unexpectedly, with his footfall smothered by the use of rubber slippers, which produced no sound. But the prisoners were able to get around him in this ruse by dropping, before they retired, small particles of coal on the floor in the passage, which crunched under his tread and thus gave ample warning of his approach.

The men engaged in boring the hole under the bed found their task seemingly interminable; but just when they began really to despair of ever penetrating the floor, which had at a certain depth changed from cement to brick, a brick suddenly fell through, leaving a considerable hole; and on widening this hole, they discovered that they had reached an air chamber running the entire length of the cells. Previous to this success, they had disposed of all the rubbish produced by the improvised chisel by hiding it carefully in the bed ticking; but afterwards, there was ample room for its concealment in the air chamber.

At the end of this chamber, they came upon a granite wall. One by one, when the presence of a single person was not so apt to be missed by the sentinel, each took up, in his turn, the task of chipping away at this solid barrier. Twenty-three days passed before the wall had been penetrated and the soft earth lying beyond it reached. They began at once to dig a tunnel, without the slightest reason to know where it would end. A whole month had been consumed when a blow of the rude instrument with which they had been so patiently excavating, opened up a ray of sunshine, and on widening the orifice, the daylight entered. But for the time being, they were not ready to escape; nor was that hour the proper one for the trial. They quietly waited until the arrival of the second night. In the meanwhile, they were very suspicious of the sentinel, and watched for his return with a feeling of acute suspense.

The afternoon preceding the night fixed for their attempt to escape having turned out to be very cloudy, they looked forward with confidence to a heavy fall of rain and more than common darkness, which they knew would make it easier for them to carry out their plan. When the sentinel entered for the last time, he handed General Morgan a letter. It ran as follows:

"My dear General – I feel certain that you are going to try

to get out of prison; but for your sake, don't you try it. You will only be taken prisoner again and made to suffer more than you do now."

The name attached to this kind and anxious note was that of a poor Irish woman whom Morgan had known in Kentucky. Was it genuine? If so, it was placed in his hands at a singular moment. Supposing that his design was suspected by friendly persons outside the walls, was this their method of setting him on the guard? The prison authorities had, of course, read the letter before it was delivered, and it must have had the effect of increasing their vigilance.

It was too late, however, to pause or take a backward step. Twelve o'clock that night had been chosen as the moment for the start. The prisoners at the usual hour were locked in the cells, and the sentinel returned later on to find out whether they were asleep in their beds; but they allowed some time to pass before they arose, for fear lest he might steal back, with the sound of his footstep carefully muffled.

Their first act was to stuff their flannel shirts with the bed clothes and to place them in the beds to simulate their bodies; the next, to descend noiselessly into the air chamber, which was now perfectly dark. The General, the last to enter, struck a match and asked in a low voice whether all the men, seven in number, were present, and whether they had ready to hand the rude cutlasses which they had, during their leisure, made out of their dinner knives. All responded in the affirmative.

It took but a minute to reach the tunnel. Everyone among them knew that the fateful moment had arrived. It was quite possible that, as soon as they issued forth, a sentinel would halt them or the prison dog betray them by baying at them. When they got out to the surface, they saw, to their delight, that rain was falling and that the night was excessively dark, in consequence of which the sentinel had retired to the shelter of his box and the dog to that of his kennel. Gliding noiselessly to the first wall, they crossed it by means of a rope ladder which they had made in prison of the sheets and blankets. At the second wall, they lifted one of their comrades on their shoulders, and he, from the top, let the rope down on the further side; but before they used it, all stopped for a few minutes in an empty sentry box to change to the civilian clothes which they had been able, through their jailor, to collect while shut up in the cells.

By the end of an hour, the time consumed in their daring enterprise, they had succeeded in getting out of the prison, and they at once broke up in groups to secure a greater chance of avoiding suspicion and escaping detection. General Morgan, with a single comrade named Hines, soon boarded a local train just about to start for Cincinnati. In taking his seat in the cars, he found next to him a Federal officer, with whom he became so genial that they exchanged drinks. As the train passed in sight of the prison where the Confederates had been so long confined, the Federal officer pointed it out to his new friend.

"There," said he, "is the hotel where that guerrilla, Morgan, and his men are spending their leisure hours."

Morgan looked at the building with great interest.

"Let us hope," he remarked drily, "that the fellow will make up his mind to board there the balance of the war, for he is a damnable nuisance."

Knowing that, before the hour the train was due to arrive at Cincinnati, the telegraph would spread far and wide the news of their escape, Morgan and Hines decided that they would jump from the car while in motion and endeavor to make their way to the Ohio river across the open country. In this manner alone could they hope to escape capture. Hines leaped and fell headlong into the ditch at the side of the roadbed. Morgan followed and struck squarely on his feet.

"What do you mean by jumping from the train," exclaimed a Federal soldier who was guarding that section of the track. His voice was gruff and his attitude threatening.

"I live here," replied Morgan quietly, "why should I go all the way to town simply to return to my home here on foot?"

The river was soon reached, and there they found a small boy in a boat apparently ready to cross.

"What are you waiting for?" asked Morgan.

"For my load. The people up yonder will soon bring it."

"What will they pay you for carrying it over?"

"Two dollars."

"Then take us over first, and we will pay you that sum."

Obtaining a horse and money, on the other side, from a lady known by them to be in sympathy with the Southern cause, they set out for Tennessee in the guise of commissaries purchasing cattle for the Federal army. In one town, they rode unchallenged through an entire regiment of the enemy which had been sent there to intercept Morgan's scattered men. Just after crossing the Tennessee river, he dismounted to rest his horse, which had become thoroughly exhausted by the rapid journey from the Ohio. He had hardly touched ground when he was fired on, but before the shot could be repeated, he had leaped into his saddle and escaped by turning immediately into the undergrowth of a neighboring mountain. Pickets were soon thrown around its base by the large Federal force which had hurried up, and there seemed to be no hope of his breaking through the cordon. That night, however, he decided that he must abandon his refuge even if he had to kill the first man who tried to stop him. Leading his horse, he quietly descended the mountain in the darkness, and coming suddenly upon a picket, was about to shoot him when he observed that he was fast asleep as he leaned heavily against a tree. Morgan lowered his pistol and passed silently on.

Stopping for rest after daylight, he found himself in front of a small, one-room farm cabin. Entering, he soon perceived that the family were Northern sympathizers. They gave him a doubly warm welcome when he told them that he was, not only a Unionist, but also a quartermaster of the Federal army who had been ordered to supply all the country people favoring the Northern cause with sugar and coffee. During this conversation, the wife of the farmer was in bed, but when she heard that they were so soon to receive a large quantity of these coveted articles, then so rarely obtained, she leaped to the floor without stopping to clothe herself more modestly.

"Thank God for that," she exclaimed, "we ain't seed any rale coffee up here since Kingdom come. I'm goin' to cook yer a fine supper right away."

"Didn't some of the rebels attempt to cross the river to-day?" asked the General, as he paused in his consumption of the excellent meal which was soon set before him on the rude table.

"That they did," cried the old woman, "and our men kilt some of um and driv' the rest away. Those that got over took to the mountains like wildcats. But they will get kilt too, for every road is watched."

"It is important for me to reach Athens tomorrow," said the General, apparently taking no notice of her remark. "If I don't, it will not be possible for me to obtain your share of that coffee and sugar. But I don't know the way and I must have a guide."

"Why, Paul," said the woman, "can't you show the Captain the path through the farm which will take him right thar whar he wants to go?"

Before the farmer could answer, Morgan turned to him and said, "The night is very cold. It is only fair I should pay you for your trouble. Here is ten dollars in gold."

The sight of the yellow metal, and the prospect of hastening the arrival of the coffee and sugar, tempted the farmer too strongly for him to resist. He rose at once to obey his wife. When Morgan parted with the countryman, he had to make his way through a region which was overrun by the Federal forces; and at one point in his road, he only escaped capture by hiding himself in the recesses of the thick undergrowth near at hand. Everywhere, he was recognized by persons who had often seen him before; but without his identity having been betrayed to the enemy on a single occasion, he arrived safely within the Confederate lines.

CHAPTER SEVEN
The Boy Artillerist

☆   ☆   ☆   ☆

If we will read the history of all great national armies, we will find that few of their officers below the rank of General have won such fame, by their skill and bravery, either in the course of one campaign or of many campaigns, that their names have become almost as renowned as the names of the commanders who directed all the manœuvres of the different divisions at the critical hour. The Army of Northern Virginia is an exception among the number. It is true that, when we recall the many triumphs of that army, it is of its three preeminent leaders, Lee, Jackson, and Stuart – the serene and far-sighted strategist, the titanic thunderbolt, and the daring cavalryman – that we first think; but as our thoughts sweep back over those fields of battle, so long deprived of all their scars by the soft touch of man and nature at peace, there rises before us a fourth figure – the figure of John Pelham, the boy artillerist, which is clothed, though in an entirely different manner, in an even finer raiment of military glory than the personalities of the three great commanders under whom he served.

Both Jackson and Stuart sank under that mortal stroke of fate which comes to all soldiers, when it does come, as a matter of course; and so did Pelham; but unlike Jackson, Stuart, and Lee, his whole military existence was literally passed in the smoke and flame of the cannon's mouth. From the moment the fighting began to the moment it ended, he was never absent from the immediate zone of the hottest firing; from the first call of the bugle, the atmosphere in which he moved was an atmosphere that fairly rocked under the terrific concussion of artillery and musketry. His duty took him at once to the border post of imminent peril, and there in the deadly breach it kept him until the wave of battle, like a wave of the sea shaken by an earthquake, had receded and died away altogether.

Imagine how supremely dauntless, how romantically brave, must have been the man who, in such an army as the Army of Northern Virginia – an army of heroes such as the world has rarely seen – was never spoken of except as the Gallant Pelham! His comrades and his countrymen did not refer to him or think of him as John Pelham, or as Major Pelham; to them, he was always the Gallant Pelham. In the midst of that host of intrepid men, he was the only one to whom this splendid popular badge of honor, as expressive as it was simple, was by common consent allowed. He had received it from General Lee himself, and it had at once been accepted by all as a just attribution to be forever coupled with his name.

Pelham was only twenty-four years of age when he was killed; and yet, as we shall see, he had, from the first great encounter of the war, although a mere boy in years as well as in appearance, been one of the strong arms on which his commanders leaned at the most critical turn of the fighting. No one thought of his youth; rather they thought of him as they would have thought of a veteran who could point to an hundred scars on his own person. It was only after his death on the battle field that the minds of men reverted to his youth.

He entered the Military Academy at West Point as a cadet from the State of Alabama when only eighteen years of age. While there, he won distinction in several ways that foreshadowed the qualities and capacities exhibited by him in the engagements of the Civil War. First of all, he was noted for his unswerving directness and perfect self-possession. It was said of him there that, whenever he crossed the parade ground, he kept to a mathematically straight line; and that the whole corps might raise a shout in his rear simultaneously, and without apparent cause, and yet he would not stop or look around to ascertain the reason for the sudden uproar.

He was very generally thought to be the most skillful athlete at the Military Academy, especially in the departments of fencing and boxing, and had hardly an equal in the exercises of the riding school. It is recorded of him that the Prince of Wales, who visited West Point in 1860, spoke with astonished admiration of his remarkable feats in horsemanship, for which he had been trained from boyhood by his life on a Southern plantation. The tradition of his extraordinary athletic and riding accomplishments lingered for many years at the Military Academy, and were among the manly memories of the great school related with undiminished enthusiasm to each successive class of "plebes."

After war broke out, Pelham offered his services to the Confederacy, and at an early date was placed in charge of the ordnance concentrated at the start at Lynchburg. This duty, imposed on him on the threshold of his career, shaped the whole of its subsequent course – he became an officer of artillery at the beginning, and remained in that arm of the service until his last hour.

When the Confederate army, under Beauregard, was gathering in the vicinity of Manassas, in expectation of McDowell's advance, Pelham was busy with all the energy and ardor of his temper, in drilling the members of Alberti's Battery, encamped near Winchester many miles away; but before the smoke began to float over the battle field on the banks of Bull Run, he had arrived at the front; where he hurried to take up with his guns a forward position so fully exposed to fire that a distinguished officer, who had accompanied him so far, quickly rode away, with the remark, "If you are fool enough to stay here, I am not." So fearless was Pelham's conduct during this battle, the first in which he had taken part, and so skillfully did he handle his guns, that he at once drew on himself the eyes of Stuart; indeed, so deeply impressed was that commander with his success as an officer under such a supreme test that he entrusted him, after the victory had been won, with the organization of a battery to consist of six pieces of Horse Artillery.

The men whom Pelham picked out to make up this battery, which, in time, came to be the most famous in the Army of Northern Virginia, were principally chosen from the regiments furnished by the State of Alabama. Some of these cannoneers had been recruited in the neighborhood of his home in that State, and had personally known him from childhood. One of the guns, which soon won a general reputation for the efficiency with which it was worked, was always loaded and fired by French Creoles from Mobile. Pelham named them his "Napoleon Detachment." They disclosed their French sympathies and emotions by singing the Marseillaise whenever they went into battle.

This was the first conspicuous scene in Pelham's career. The battery which he now organized was the nucleus of the celebrated batteries of horse artillery which formed so invaluable a section of Stuart's command, and shared, either partly or wholly under Pelham's direction, in all the principal battles in which the officer was engaged. He was perhaps the youngest man to hold so important a position in this arm of the Confederate service. He was still a boy in appearance as well as in years.

The daring which he displayed at First Manassas was to be repeated on every field on which he fought thereafter; it was noted that, as soon as the enemy began retiring, his guns were rushed far ahead of the Confederate infantry to shell the retreating ranks; and that, whenever the cavalry at full tilt went into action, these guns accompanied them at the same high rate of speed. The horse artillery always entered a battle at a gallop; it withdrew at a snail's pace. In the course of the fighting, Pelham is said to have shown the gayety of a school boy on the playground; and he frequently spoke of a battle where he had been more reckless than usual in exposing himself to danger as a "jolly good fight."

When the Confederate army, after Manassas, fell back from the general line of the Rappahannock, to Pelham was assigned the supreme duty of guarding the rear against concentrated attack, and of closing the fords to prevent the enemy's passage until the main force had got well away. This duty he performed successfully.

The next battle in which he was actually engaged was the Battle of Williamsburg, which General Johnston fought while retreating from the entrenchments around Yorktown; and so inspiring was Pelham's example on this field that it was said at the time that he had, by his skill and intrepidity, "converted raw militia into veterans." At Cold Harbor, in the course of the Seven Days' Campaign, he advanced one piece of artillery under his own personal direction fully one third of a mile ahead of the Confederate position. During an hour, this was the only gun of the Confederate right wing that was firing; and it held its place although the shells of an entire Federal battery were discharged against it.

So soon as the battle of Second Manassas opened, he pushed his battery at a gallop into the midst of the sharpshooters thrown out in front of the Federal army; nor did he order the horses to be halted until the guns had come almost up to the line of the massed columns. As Stonewall Jackson looked on at the cannoneers, so dangerously posted and yet firing into the ranks of the enemy as coolly as if from some distant hill, he said to Stuart, in his dry, laconic way, "If you have another Pelham, give him to me."

At Sharpsburg, Pelham had charge of most of the artillery operating on the Confederate right wing, which was under the command of Stonewall Jackson in person. So incessantly did his guns roar, so much daring did he display in advancing them, and so efficiently did he work them, that Jackson, who was rarely given to bursts of praise and who was one of the least impulsive of men, exclaimed, "Every army should have a Pelham on each flank."

And when General Lee abandoned the heights of Antietam and passed across the Potomac to the Virginia side, Pelham posted his horse artillery opposite the ford at Shepherdstown, perhaps the most vital of all the fords, and held back the enemy with a firmness and tenacity which they found it impossible to break down; and he only retired at last when further resistance had been made unnecessary by the safe withdrawal of the Confederate troops in the direction of Winchester.

An interval of rest and recuperation for the Confederate and Federal armies now followed, during which, in the beautiful home of friends on the banks of the Opequan, Pelham passed the last autumn of his life. There he renewed, under the magnificent oaks and sycamores that surrounded the house, that love of nature and natural scenery which he had first acquired amid the scenes of his early boyhood in Alabama. He found great pleasure too in wandering alone through the distant woods and fields. In his intercourse with his friends under this hospitable roof-tree, he revealed more conspicuously than ever that sweetness of temper, simplicity of character, and courtesy of manner, which had always seemed to those who knew him well to set off so beautifully the stern underlying qualities of his nature as exhibited in the flame and smoke of battle.

But in the midst of the happiness of this peaceful rural seat, his thoughts were never long turned away from the enemy, who were now encamped in Virginia, and were expected to move at an early day. From the hour when Burnside began to descend from Aldie, on the east side of the Blue Ridge Mountains, he found Pelham's artillery hotly and pertinaciously disputing every foot of his progress towards the Rappahannock. So resolute and fearless was Pelham, in fact, that quite often he would not draw back until the foe had come up to a point that appeared to be only a few feet from the muzzle of his most forward gun.

On a certain day, he had pushed one piece of his artillery very much ahead of the rest, and it was in imminent danger of being captured; the enemy, indeed, were marching straight up to it. At this critical moment, Pelham was handed an order from Stuart to fall back. So hot was the fire that his men had already retired precipitately from the ground, but he lingered for a few minutes longer alone. He loaded the piece himself and set it off, apparently in the very face of the attacking force; then he quietly mounted one of the wheel horses and started all four off with the gun at a gallop. A fusillade followed him, and the horse he rode fell in his tracks; he instantly cut the traces, and mounting the other wheel horse, started off a second time at a gallop with the gun. The second horse, like the first, was soon shot and disabled; again he cut the traces, and mounting one of the two leaders, started off the third time at a gallop. The third horse also was in a few minutes struck to the ground; not hesitating one moment, he cut the traces of this horse, and mounting the fourth and last, succeeded in rushing the gun off the field without any mishap either to it or himself.

It was probably during these operations on the Rappahannock that a stirring scene which revealed the celerity, efficiency, and fearlessness of Pelham's battery occurred. It was witnessed by a Confederate officer who had fallen a prisoner in the hands of the enemy. A stream ran between the lines of the two armies. On the Confederate side, a road which wound behind the rampart of broken hills abutting on the bank of this stream, was, from the Federal position opposite, exposed to full view for the space of two hundred yards. Down this highway, a long Confederate wagon train was compelled to pass, and while they were fully protected during the time they were screened by the hills, they were in immediate danger of destruction from the fire of a powerful Federal battery just as soon as they emerged to sight in the open section of the road. Before reaching this section, each driver, by terrific blows of his heavy whip, would start his mules off at top speed; and standing up in his stirrups, hallooing in his loudest voice, and continuing to flog with all his might, would endeavor to rush his clumsy wagon unharmed along the unsheltered part of the road to the security of the hill at the other end. As each wagon came into view, the Federal battery would discharge a round of shrieking shells at the rapidly moving target, with the natural effect of further hastening the pace of the frightened driver and his mules.

About a quarter of a mile back of the first line of hills, there rose another and a higher line, with their top covered with a dense growth of trees; but, on the side that fell away to the hollow between the two ridges, entirely clear of forest. Just at the time when the Federal battery was about to direct an increased fire at the open section of the road, two pieces of horse artillery belonging to Pelham's battery galloped out of the bosom of the wood growing on the second ridge and began to descend along the bare slope at the same high rate of speed. Disappearing from sight in the bottom, they reappeared on the top of the line of hills, overlooking the river, which confronted the position of the Federal battery. The horses, straining at their harness, continued to advance at a gallop, with the cannoneers either bestriding them or clinging to those parts of the guns where they could find a footing.

Suddenly, the horses were halted, and the men leaped to the ground and began to ram the loads into the muzzles. Hardly a minute seemed to pass before there was a puff of white smoke; the roar of an explosion followed, and simultaneously a bolt struck one of the cannon of the Federal battery. A second shell shrieked from the other Confederate gun almost at the same instant; a third, a fourth, a fifth – all of which reached their mark or rebounded very close to it.

So astonished at first were the Federal cannoneers that it was not until the sixth shell had been fired by the two puny Confederate guns that the Federal battery responded; and when it did reply, although this battery was opposing as many as six guns to two, it was unable to discharge a greater number of shells than its small Confederate rival. At last outmatched, in spite of its superior weight in metal, it withdrew out of range and declined to exchange further shots at all.

But the most celebrated exploit in the military career of Pelham was yet to occur; and this exploit, as we shall see, was entirely in harmony with that spirit of reckless daring which he had already displayed so many times in the forefront of the battle field. The great armies of Burnside and Lee had taken their respective positions on the opposite heights looking down on the Rappahannock at Fredericksburg. The hills on the north bank of the river were crowned with earthworks as a bulwark for a long line of Federal batteries, which were ready at the word of command to hurl thousands of shells across the broad plain spread out between the two hostile forces. The stream ran at the base of these fortified hills, and from its southern bank the lowland rolled away to the foot of the high ground where the entrenched Confederate army awaited the onset of the foe. Burnside had decided to throw his troops across the Rappahannock by means of pontoon bridges, and under the protection of the guns on the heights behind them, to march them straight over this plain to attack the Confederate position.

It was the morning of December 13th, 1862. A heavy fog veiled the surface of the valley and hid from view the divisions of the enemy, which had crossed the stream at an early hour and been drawn up by their officers in battle array on the south bank while they were still invisible.

Lee, Jackson, and Stuart about this time mounted their horses and rode down behind the line of Confederate bayonets. Stuart, when they arrived near the spot where his artillery was stationed, quietly beckoned to Pelham, and on his quickly coming up, gave him an order in a low voice. Pelham, having saluted, returned to his post, and in a few minutes was to be seen galloping down towards the plain, followed by his Napoleon gun manned by his French Creole cannoneers. This gun had been captured at Cold Harbor in the campaign of the Seven Days Battles; and it had thundered louder than any other in his battery in the hottest fighting at Second Manassas, Sharpsburg, and Aldie.

Pelham, had he preferred, could have sent one of his officers to discharge the duty which Stuart had imposed, but the task was one peculiarly agreeable to him as it gave him another chance to rush his Napoleon ahead of his own columns into the very teeth of the enemy. The position which he now took up was far out on the plain and in the very path of the approaching Federal army; and he made himself the most conspicuous target by keeping his seat on horseback at the very moment he was forcing his men to lie down.

At first, the blanket of mist was so thick that the only proof of the enemy's presence was given by the music of the military bands that accompanied the different corps. Gradually, the fog lifted as the rays of the morning sun grew warmer, and a magnificent and most formidable spectacle was revealed to the eyes of the waiting cannoneers. A vast host of blue-coats, marshaled in battle line, with their starry flags held aloft, and their bayonets rising like a forest above their heads, and their metal accoutrements glittering in the light, were marching forward with a steady tramp which resounded even from that distance.

Here were but a single gun and a handful of cannoneers in the very path of this mighty army. The only possible supporters of these brave men were entrenched far behind on the southern heights; and to make their situation the more precarious, the batteries on the north side of the Rappahannock began to hurl a hurricane of shells in every direction over that part of the plain which spread out ahead of the advancing Federal columns.

Pelham's gun faced the left wing of the Federal hosts, composed of Meade's Division. Just as soon as it came in range, he opened a rapid fire on its ranks; and he kept this up until Doubleday's Division, wheeling to the left, marched to its assistance. He continued to pour one shrieking shell after another into this reinforced mass; and at last it recoiled in confusion; but soon reformed and came on again. His single gun was now exposed to the concentrated fire of at least five battalions attached to these two Federal Divisions. Amidst the tremendous roar that was shaking earth and sky, the Creole cannooneers could be heard singing the Marseillaise as blithely as if they were taking part in some grand review, while Pelham calmly continued to give his orders from the saddle.

All this time, the entire Confederate army posted on the hills, and a large part of the Federal on the plain, were looking on at the duel going on with such odds against the youthful artillerist.

"It is glorious," exclaimed General Lee, giving voice to his admiration, "to see such courage in one so young."

During an entire hour, Pelham stopped the enemy's advance; and he finally drew off only on receiving a peremptory order from Stuart to retire, as General Lee, who knew that the

Poured one shrieking shell after another into this mass.

gun's resistance must, in the end, give way before the joint impact of Meade and Doubleday, preferred that these Divisions should now move on to the assault of the heights, where his forces were impatiently awaiting them. The favorable issue of the battle could be promoted but not brought about by one such act of extraordinary bravery.

Retreating to the hills, Pelham took command of all the artillery posted on the Confederate right wing, and had charge of it until night fell. As the Federals, discomfited, slowly withdrew, he steadily pushed forward his guns; and they were thundering away as long as there was light enough to take accurate aim.

During the winter, the two armies remained inactive; but in March (1863), Averill crossed the Rappahannock at Kelly's Ford, not far from Fredericksburg, at the head of three thousand cavalrymen. It happened that Pelham had accompanied Stuart to a camp some distance away to attend a court martial, and while returning, heard the boom of cannon in the direction of the river; he immediately galloped forward; and when he reached the scene of fighting, his own artillery not yet having come upon the ground, he observed a regiment which appeared to be severely shaken by the hot fire suddenly concentrated on its ranks. He galloped up to the men, and waving his hat, shouted out, "Form, Boys. Forward to victory and glory."

He had hardly uttered these brave words when he fell headlong from his horse. A fragment of shell had struck him on the head, a blow which proved to be fatal at the end of a few hours. His body was taken to Richmond, and lay in state there in the capitol as if his part in the war had been as important as that of some commanding General.

Never before or afterwards, during the course of the great conflict, did the death of so young an officer call forth such a eulogistic proclamation as the one which Stuart issued to his men when told that Pelham had been killed.

"To you, his comrades, it is needless to dwell upon what you have so often witnessed – his prowess in action, already proverbial. You well know how, though young in years, a mere stripling in appearance, remarkable for his genuine modesty of deport-ment, he yet disclosed on the battlefield the conduct of a veteran, and displayed in his handsome person the most imperturbable coolness in danger. His eye had glanced over every battle field of this army, from First Manassas to the moment of his death, and he was, with a single exception, a brilliant actor in them all. The memory of the gallant Pelham, his many virtues, his noble nature, and purity of character, is enshrined as a sacred legacy in the hearts of all who knew him. His record has been bright and spot-less; his career brilliant and successful. He fell – the noblest of sacrifices on the altar of his country, to whose glorious service he had dedicated his life from the beginning of the war."

CHAPTER EIGHT
Mosby and the Partisan Rangers

☆   ☆   ☆   ☆

The most famous of all the partisan rangers of the South, during the Civil War, was Colonel Mosby, whose exploits in that character are more like the inventions of some stirring writer of romance than events of history that really took place. He entered upon the scenes of this part of his career – he had been a simple scout before – while still a young man, full of the adventurous spirit which is youth's sharpest spur to energetic and daring action. His person is thrown against the screen of those extraordinary times as boldly as if he stood in the very first rank of its greatest soldiers; one can see in the mind's eye, with all the distinctness of actual vision, his slender, almost gaunt, figure, his beardless lip, his tanned cheek, and his piercing eye, before which the most reckless of his followers who had given offense was forced to quail. He wears a gray uniform, and the only weapons which he carries are the two pistols that are stuck in his belt.

A quiet, reticent, and withal a stern man, he was unbending in compelling the fullest obedience to all his orders; and yet he never for a moment relaxed the vigilance of his eye for the safety and comfort of his soldiers; and on no occasion would he command them to go where he was not willing to lead.

Being an unerring judge of character, he refused to accept as a member of his band anyone who did not win his confidence at once, a matter of vital importance in the peculiar kind of warfare in which he was engaged. In fact, he had an unalterable conviction as to the sort of men that he needed; and he declined to allow the mere appeals of personal liking to influence him in his choice; sometimes, indeed, as we shall see, he admitted to his squad men who, in the beginning, were looked upon by all its members, except himself, as disguised spies, but who, by their fidelity and loyalty, proved the correctness of his instinctive faith in their trustworthiness.

The fame of Colonel Mosby will always be associated with that part of Piedmont, Virginia which lies between the upper waters of the Potomac and those of the Rappahannock, with the cloud-capped wall of the Blue Ridge as its western boundary. This region was as much a debatable land during the Civil War as the romantic borders of Scotland in the days of the Highlander forays and English raids – a land which belonged to that army of either side which could hold it for a day, or a month, or a year. But Mosby and his partisan rangers considered it to be their own; and not the less so when the Federal troops happened to be in seemingly indisputable possession of its grass-covered hills and valleys, and its dense and dark woods.

The counties of Loudon and Fairfax particularly were known as Mosby's Confederacy. This was, indeed, a region which was precisely suited in all its features to the operations of a partisan force; for, being beautifully pastoral, it overflowed with those supplies for man and beast which such a force were compelled to pick up as they stole or hurried from point to point; and it also contained thick bodies of forest to serve as a screen in excursions against the enemy or as a hiding place whenever discretion suggested a temporary retreat before superior numbers. Besides, it spread right up to the base of the Blue Ridge, in the fastnesses of which the entire company could withdraw in safety when the season or hot pursuit dictated their complete dissolution and dispersion.

The rangers were kept together only when Mosby was engaged in some one of his furtive expeditions. If there was no

raid underway, either because the period of the year was unfavor-
able or the enemy were too cautious to offer a vulnerable side, his
men were widely scattered among the homes of the small farmers
who lived in the more or less remote and inaccessible foot hills of
the Blue Ridge. Here they were able to obtain comforts which
were not customary either with themselves or with the soldiers of
the main armies when on the march or in camp or bivouac. The
food set before them by their rural hosts was abundant and whole-
some, although plain and without much variety; there was plenty
of cornbread, bacon, poultry, game, and vegetables to appease
their hunger from day to day; and they had clean shuck mattresses
and substantial beds to sleep on at night; while for their horses,
whose good condition was of as much concern to them as their
own, the blue grass in the meadows and on the hillsides, and the
grain and hay in the stables, afforded all the provender that they
required to keep them sleek, fat, and hardy.

Mosby had established his secret headquarters in the little
town of Upperville not far off, and when, by the report of his
scouts or by his own personal observations – for he frequently
ventured alone into the neighborhood of the enemy's encampments – he saw an opportunity to deliver a sudden but furtive
blow, he dispatched a mounted courier to the nearest locality in
the foothills of the mountains where he knew that some of his
band were awaiting his summons; in turn, one of this number was
instructed to take horse and to carry the same summons to the
next locality; and so on, until all the rangers had received the order
to assemble at the rendezvous, often forty or fifty miles away,
which had been specially appointed by their leader.

Whoever failed to obey this order without having a good
excuse, was promptly and peremptorily commanded to go back to
the company in the regular army from which he had been detailed;
but it was very rare, indeed, that a trooper turned a deaf ear to the
call; in fact, a lazy life in the farmers' houses lost all its charms so
soon as the prospect of taking part in some adventurous raid was
held out to him by the courier's announcement. He was clearly
aware that Mosby would not have sent for him had he not already

matured some daring excursion which would afford his men, in carrying it out, plenty of glorious excitement.

Twenty-four hours had hardly passed when the Partisan Chief would find himself surrounded at the rendezvous by twenty, thirty, and sometimes fifty soldiers, burning to follow him even to the death, without thinking it necessary first to request him to reveal his plans or his destination. Who were these troopers who gathered around Mosby as quickly and excitedly as a pack of buckhounds run together about their huntsman when he sounds the first note on his familiar horn?

The majority were young men of adventurous and even reckless spirit who had obtained permission to leave the ranks of Stuart's command in order to join the Partisan Leader; a few were hardly more than boys, who had never served under any other officer or in any other troop; one or two were soldiers of fortune, attracted to him from oversea by his reputation for splendid daring, which had spread even to those distant parts.

There was not one who did not ride with the skill of a Mexican herdsman, and who did not feel rather more at home in the saddle than on the ground. If there was no reason at the moment for silence and vigilance, they showed the gayety and buoyancy of their spirits as they rode along by trolling the songs which were popular with the cavalry.

Ordinarily, Mosby's rangers wore no uniform, but they were always distinguishable as Confederate soldiers by some badge of grayness about their clothes. After a successful raid, as was said at the time, they were the best equipped, best mounted, and best dressed men in their arm of the service; the dandies among them would then show themselves in suits remarkable for gold braid, buff trimmings, and gilt buttons; would wear high-topped boots and soft hats decorated with glossy ostrich plumes. These splendid garments and trappings were quickly discarded on the first news of the enemy's presence.

There were few features of their daily life when actually in the field which recalled the routine of the regular soldiers, whether in camp or on the march – for instance, they were never awakened at dawn by the reveille; they were not required at night to retire to sleep by the sounding of taps; there was rarely a roll call to show presence or absence; and there was never a drill. No supply of food, clothes, ammunition, or guns was ever given out to them; they picked up their rations in the countryside as they passed along; and the remainder they obtained by capture. They never slept under a tent; when they wanted rest at night, they stretched themselves on the ground wrapped in their blankets, while their horses either stood picketed close by or were allowed to graze in the nearest field until the eastern sky showed the approach of dawn.

It was not simply a spirit of aimless daring that influenced Mosby even in his most reckless adventures. He had invariably certain definite purposes to carry through. The principal one always was to find out the movements of the enemy and to fathom their designs, with the view of reporting them for the guidance of Lee and Stuart. Subordinate to this, he sought to harass and worry the enemy's detachments; to cut the telegraph wires and break up the railroads within their lines; to capture dispatches passing to and from the hostile headquarters; to destroy wagon trains loaded with army supplies; to seize pickets, scouts, and videttes; and to overrun isolated camps.

He was always looking for and trying to strike at unprotected gaps on the hostile front or rear in order to force the enemy to use up a great many troops in guarding all points; and he was indefatigable in his efforts to disrupt their communications by every means available to his hand. So suddenly did he appear in the open, so quickly did he vanish in the nearest forest, that he was often spoken of by the foe as the Flying Dutchman of the Woods, and his followers as Children of the Mist.

CHAPTER NINE
Capture of General Stoughton

☆　　☆　　☆　　☆

Perhaps the most brilliant of all Mosby's exploits as a partisan ranger was his capture of General Stoughton in March, 1863. At this time, he had under his command a small band of carefully picked troopers. The Fifth New York Cavalry Regiment and other Federal forces were now encamped near Fairfax Court-House, and it was important that their movements should be followed and their designs, if possible, penetrated. Mosby was debating in his own mind as to the most practicable means of obtaining the information desired, when a deserter from the enemy appeared in the circle of his bivouac and expressed an earnest wish to join his company. At first, this man, whose name was Ames, was looked upon by the rangers with strong suspicion as a possible spy, and his presence was barely tolerated; but Mosby, after carefully weighing all his assertions about himself, and for some time observing his bearing, decided to permit him to remain, a conclusion which he never had reason to regret, for Ames became one of the most daring and trustworthy of his squad; was promoted to a lieutenancy; and finally perished in a hand-to-hand combat with one of the enemy's cavalrymen.

When Ames entered the rangers' camp, it happened that there was one among them who was anxious to procure a horse before the expedition which he knew was on foot should set out.

How was he to supply his want in time? If he failed to secure a horse, he would be left behind, and would thus miss all the certain excitement, and his share in the possible profits, of the projected adventure. Ames too was without a horse, and when told by the ranger of his own necessity, he thought that he saw an opportunity to obtain steeds for both, and, in doing so, to win at one stroke the unreserved confidence of his new comrades.

"If you will go with me," he said, "I will take you to the camp where I was stationed, and there I feel sure we can each lay hands on a horse."

It seemed to be full of risk to rely so far on a deserter's word as to accompany him to the very spot from which he had fled. What if he should after all turn out to be a spy? But the trooper was so eager to obtain a horse, that, after a moment's hesitation, he agreed to adopt Ames's suggestion. Leaving the rangers' bivouac, they made their way through the woods to the enemy's nearest encampment, which they reached at midnight, when only the sentinels were awake. These sentinels knew Ames personally, and he was confident that, if they were unaware of his desertion, which he thought probable, they would permit him and his companion to enter the bounds after a curt challenge. And in this anticipation, he proved to be right; the first sentinel they came upon, on being told his name, offered no objection; and the two men immediately found themselves within the limits of the enemy's post. Ames and his comrade went straight to the spot where the horses were tethered, and after looking them over as carefully as the darkness allowed, each mounted the particular animal which he preferred and rode away. The sentinel took them to be merely pickets going to relieve others who had been watching during the first part of the night.

Mosby had made up his mind to penetrate as far within the Federal lines as Fairfax Court-House; and this successful adventure of the two men confirmed him in his purpose. It proved that Ames could be fully trusted; and with the advantage of Ames's minute knowledge of the Federal camps, he felt more confident that the projected dash could be triumphantly carried out. The objective which he had in view was not disclosed to any of his men; they were only aware that some excursion more daring even than usual was in contemplation, and they were entirely content to repress their curiosity. Mosby really designed, not only to pass straight through the Federal lines, but also to bring off General Stoughton, who was stationed at Fairfax Court House. This would be a blow that would resound like a thunderclap, and would give him such a reputation at a single stroke that his success in his future enterprises would certainly be promoted by it. Not only did he have among his followers the deserter Ames, who was thoroughly informed as to all the camps of the enemy, but also two brothers, Underwood by name, who were said to know every natural feature of all that region as well as did the animals that prowled by day or night about its fields and woods. Having explored every swamp and every forest situated in Fairfax county, they would be able to guide the rangers by paths which the Federal troops were ignorant of, although not far away from the localities where they were stationed.

It would be hard to imagine a more difficult or a more adventurous enterprise than Mosby was now about to start upon. Fairfax Court-House, his destination, not only itself was occupied by Federal soldiers, but in its immediate vicinity two infantry regiments were encamped. Three regiments of cavalry, under Colonel Wyndham, an English officer, were stationed within three miles of the town; and at Centreville, not far off, there was posted an infantry brigade; while at Fairfax station, two miles to the south, a second brigade of infantry was to be found. Thus there stood between Mosby and his prey a most formidable mass of cavalry, infantry, and artillery.

There were three highways leading to Fairfax Court-House from the west and south, from which directions alone would Mosby be able to approach. If he went all the way by the Little River turnpike, he would be certain to run up against Colonel Wyndham's cavalry; should he choose the Warrenton turnpike, he would eventually find himself face to face with a mixed force of cavalry, infantry, and artillery. On the other hand, if he advanced by the railway, he would be halted by the brigade at Fairfax station before he could debouch into the road running to the Court-House.

He finally decided to seek a door through the cordon by stealing down the body of woods that lay in the triangle between the Little River and Warrenton turnpikes, with its apex pointing to the Court-House. There were twenty-nine men in the band that followed him when he set out for his dangerous objective. All were mounted on strong and well trained horses. When they started down the Little River turnpike, which they had to travel along at first, night had fallen and the darkness seemed to wrap every object in pitchy blackness. On arriving at a point about three miles from the hamlet of Chantilly, they turned off the highway and entered the thick wood that tapered towards the Court-House. The darkness grew more dense than ever in the recesses of the forest; and in a short time, the two squads, into which the men had been divided, became separated. The second squad began to stumble aimlessly about among the trees, perplexed as to which was the right direction to take, while the first went forward without any suspicion that their comrades had lost the track. Some of the men of the second squad, having no guides and becoming discouraged, proposed that they should endeavor to find their way back to the camp which they had so recently left; some suggested that they should remain where they were until Mosby, missing them, should send the two Underwood scouts to bring them up. On the other hand, the majority urged that they should go straight on in the hope of recovering the trail of the first squad. This advice in the end prevailed. Reaching an opening in the forest, they saw a light shining through an open window, and on riding up to inquire as to their whereabouts, they, to their relief, discovered Mosby and the other members of the advance squad seated within. The rangers had now reached the outer line of the Federal pickets, and it was only by observing the utmost caution, aided by the pall of darkness, that they succeeded in creeping through the cordon without having been detected. Fairfax Court-House was situated about four miles away. They now turned towards the turnpike that passed from the Court-House through Centreville westward; entering it, they cut the wires, and, at a rapid trot, advanced down the highway until they began to draw near to the camp where a large body of Federal troops were posted. Here they were within one and a half miles of the Court-House. Leaving the enemy's station on their left, the rangers boldly struck into the thick woods again.

It was Mosby's aim now to reach the road running from the Court-House to Fairfax station, which he knew to be unprotected, except at the station itself, by any force stronger than pickets, who might be easily captured if they should attempt to block his path. Debouching into this road after their passage of the woods, the rangers turned their horses' heads straight towards the village, which they entered at two o'clock in the morning. A profound silence hung over the place. Not a dog bayed at them as they rode up; not a cock was heard to crow; citizens, dogs, and chickens alike seemed to be buried in the deepest slumber.

The cavalcade drew rein in the Court-House square. No word was spoken above a whisper. Mosby ordered Ames, the Federal deserter, and one ranger besides to dismount and remain there, while the rest of the company, headed by himself, went to the home of a citizen who was personally known to him as an ardent supporter of the Southern cause. During the short interval of waiting, a sentinel came up to Ames and his companion.

"What are you doing here?" he asked abruptly.

"I belong to the Fifth New York Cavalry Regiment," replied Ames, coolly, "and I am waiting here by order of Major White, whom I am expecting any moment."

The answer quieted the suspicions of the sentinel, and he was about to pass on, when Ames, as if to whisper in his ear, leaned forward in the darkness and suddenly grasped his gun.

"If you utter a sound," he exclaimed in a low voice, "you are a dead man."

The sentinel was so astonished that he was quickly disarmed and taken prisoner.

Hardly had this incident concluded, when Mosby returned

with his men to the square. He divided them at once into three squads; one was dispatched to the stables to bring off the finest horses of the officers; another to the headquarters of Colonel Wyndham to capture him; while Colonel Mosby, accompanied by two rangers, walked over to the house occupied by General Stoughton.

To Ames was assigned the duty of seizing Colonel Wyndham, but he was found to have left the village on a visit to Washington. While Ames himself was searching that officer's bedchamber, his comrades were exploring another, where they pulled out of his hiding place a Federal, who earnestly represented himself to be a common sutler, and therefore, too unimportant to be carried off a prisoner; but Ames, on entering the room, recognized him as Captain Barker, who was in command of the company to which he had belonged before his desertion. Barker at once gave himself up without offering further protest.

The squad that was sent to the stable led to the square, within a few minutes, a string of fine horses, fully saddled and bridled.

But Mosby's own experience was the most dramatic of the night. On reaching General Stoughton's headquarters, he found that his bedroom was situated up-stairs. The doors to both floors were unlocked; and so complete was the General's sense of security that no sentinel was posted either within or without the house. Quietly entering his chamber, Mosby found him fast asleep in bed. Going up to its side, he slapped the slumbering officer's shoulder so heavily that he awoke; but at first he was in a state of dumb, bewildered surprise at the sight that was presented to his eyes. He slowly raised himself on his elbow and scowled at the intruder.

"What is the meaning of this visit at such an hour?" he at last growled out.

"Get up, I want you," was the short reply.

General Stoughton looked at Mosby with a blacker scowl on his face.

"Do you know who I am," he gruffly demanded. "I will have you arrested."

"Do you know who I am?" retorted Mosby coolly.

"Who are you?"

"Did you ever hear of Mosby?"

"Yes, have you got him?"

"No, but he has got you."

"What does all this mean, Sir?" cried Stoughton indignantly.

"Mean," said Mosby, quietly, "why it means that Stuart's cavalry are in possession of the town, and you are a prisoner. Get up and accompany me."

General Stoughton's body-guard, consisting of two soldiers, occupied a tent at the back of the house, and like their master, they were taken fast asleep, for they also thought that there was no necessity for watchfulness.

Stoughton having been required to dress quickly and descend, Mosby and his two men, with their captives, returned to the square, where the other squads had already arrived with fifty-eight of the officers' saddle horses and thirty-two prisoners. They had been busy in the village for one hour and a half, and it would not be long before the first signs of dawn would appear in the sky. The captives having been quickly mounted, the whole cavalcade was on the point of leaving the place behind when the sound of a window sash being thrown up was heard.

"What cavalry is that?" a voice called out.

A smothered laugh was the only reply.

"Dismount, Nelson and Hatcher," Mosby ordered in low tones, "and search that house."

The two men, on entering the principal room in the building, found it occupied by an officer's wife in bed; on a chair nearby was a Colonel's uniform; on the table, his hat; and hanging on the wall, his gold watch. The officer himself, suspecting that there was something wrong, had escaped in his night clothes into the garden, and thence into the dark fields beyond. Time was too valuable to justify his further pursuit, for, should Mosby not succeed in passing the picket line before daylight, the alarm would be given and his whole band intercepted.

Taking the open road to Fairfax station, previously used by them, the rangers branched off into the woods so soon as they reached the spot where they had entered the highway a few hours before, and rode straight towards Centreville. Not far from that place, they had to make a detour to avoid the brigade of cavalry posted there; and in doing this, they passed so close to a strong Federal fortification that a sentinel challenged them; but they hurried on without replying. Captain Barker took advantage of the proximity of Federal soldiers to endeavor to escape. The ball fired at him as he started to gallop away in their direction just grazed his head, and he was quickly recaptured.

Having got by the fortifications in safety, Mosby and his men soon arrived on the banks of Cub Run, which they found very much swollen from the melting snows in the foothills of the mountains. Without the slightest hesitation, they plunged into the racing stream. Mosby himself led the way and General Stoughton followed close behind him. When the latter reached land again, he said jocularly to his captor, "This is the first bad treatment I have received from you. Colonel." Many of the men were carried down the stream, but, in the end, succeeded in scrambling up the bank and joining their comrades.

When they drew near to Groveton, Mosby, accompanied by one of his men, galloped to the top of a hill commanding a view of the region rolling away towards Centreville, which he had just traversed with the prisoners and his own band. Not a horseman, not an infantryman, not a battery, was in sight; the pursuit had evidently been considered useless and had not been undertaken.

Mosby delivered his captives to the Confederate authorities at Culpeper Court-House, where General Fitzhugh Lee was in command. Lee had been a classmate of Stoughton at the West Point Military Academy, and received the distinguished prisoner with every mark of consideration.

The raid upon the village did not become generally known to the Federals at Fairfax Court-House until the next morning, and as it seemed impossible for even Mosby to have carried it out so successfully without local connivance, eight of the leading citizens of the place were arrested and thrown into the Old Capitol Prison at Washington. As for Mosby himself, the astonishing daring which he had shown and its triumphant issue, established his reputation as the most brilliant partisan leader in the Eastern theatre of the war; and this reputation his subsequent exploits served to confirm.

CHAPTER TEN
The Wagon Train and Greenback Raids

☆   ☆   ☆   ☆

The final summer of the war had arrived, and the Valley of Virginia was once more to become the field on which Federal and Confederate armies were to clash for mastery; that region had been the scene of some of the first battles of the great conflict, and it was now to be the scene of some of the last. Here the only remaining hope of establishing Southern independence was to vanish, for, when General Early's surviving soldiers, travel-stained and war-worn, were dispersed, there was left no reasonable ground for thinking that General Lee, in the trenches of Petersburg, could continue to hold his lines in the teeth of the increase in the numbers of his Federal adversaries which must quickly follow.

In August, 1864, General Sheridan, who was to strike so many vigorous blows at the Confederates operating between the Alleghanies and the Blue Ridge, took command at Harper's Ferry of all the Federal troops posted in that region. There was at least one eagle eye that was turned to watch his movements intently from the moment when he began to show the first sign of activity. This was Mosby's. At daybreak one morning in August, he set out from a rendezvous east of the mountains for the Shenandoah Valley, at the head of three hundred rangers, who had been hardened in body and spirit by the adventurous life led by them during the seventeen months that had passed since their chief had broken into the village of Fairfax Court-House at night and carried off General Stoughton and his comrades. After a long and fatiguing march through the foothills and defiles of the Blue Ridge, the band halted, just as darkness came on, at a spot situated not far from the little town of Berryville, and almost within arm's reach of Harper's Ferry itself.

The men brought no encumbering tents with them, and they made no effort to seek the shelter of houses; they simply unsaddled their bespattered and hungry horses and turned them out to crop the grass, while they stretched themselves on the turf to snatch a few hours' sleep before again taking up the search for the enemy.

So soon as they lay down to rest and recuperate, scouts were dispatched into the surrounding region to find out whether there were any Federal detachments abroad there, either quietly encamped, scouring the country for prisoners, or spying out for information. They returned almost at once and reported that the very largest wagon train of the enemy which they had ever seen in the course of the whole war, was moving, like a great procession, along the Valley turnpike, situated behind a ridge of low hills rising a short distance away.

Mosby, on being told of this welcome fact, picked out half a dozen members of his band to accompany him in his first reconnoissance; the others he ordered to remain where they were until he should send them word to join him at the scene of the proposed attack. Even in this exciting moment, he was anxious that they should not be disturbed in their repose until the need of their assistance became immediate.

As he and his companions cautiously advanced under the cover of darkness, they could distinctly hear the rumble of hundreds of wheels, the sharp cracking of numerous whips, and the curses and the songs of the drivers. The bed of the turnpike being of macadamized stone, and the air being still, the roll of so many wagons passing over so hard a surface was borne far and wide through the sleeping country. The sound fell very pleasantly on the ears of the listening Confederate troopers, for they were able to gauge by its volume how immense would be the damage which they would soon be able to inflict on the enemy.

All the rangers, including Mosby, were dressed in the civilian clothes of common Virginian farmers. When they walked right up to the turnpike and got their first view of the strung-out wagon train, advancing like an enormous snake along the track of the winding highway – a sight which delighted their hostile eyes – they made no attempt whatever to conceal themselves beyond first breaking up their group and taking position beside the roadway in couples at points considerably apart; in fact, they appeared, as they looked on, to be simply so many rustics who had been drawn by curiosity from their homes nearby to watch so extraordinary a spectacle close at hand.

But they were not satisfied to stand long by the roadside and gaze with open mouths in pretended unsophisticated astonishment – they boldly joined the large band of camp followers and conversed with them, and also with the nearest drivers, without exciting the slightest suspicion either by their dress, words, or bearing. Indeed, it was doubtful whether, after they actually mingled with that motley assemblage, they were taken to be even strangers, for whatever in their aspect might otherwise have made them different from the rest of the crowd was more or less hidden by the shadow of night. Some of the troopers, however, did not hesitate to ask for matches and to light their pipes in the very faces of drivers and hangers-on alike. Through the latter, by apparently casual questions, they found that, in addition to the wagons and their loads, there were at least nine hundred head of horses, mules, and cattle in the train; and that they were guarded by two thousand men under the command of General Kenly. Not content with this information, the rangers wormed in and out and made a furtive, superficial inspection of the contents of the wagons; and examined in the same sly way the quality of the herd and drove of live-stock.

At last, satisfied with the facts which they had learned, either by word of mouth or by the use of their own eyes, the rangers, under orders passed by Mosby to each of his companions, fell out of the line of the wagon train and took a position hidden from observation not far from the roadside.

The first flush of morning had not yet appeared. One of the troopers was hurried off to awaken the remainder of the band, who, as has been seen, had been left behind to rest. In addition to the three hundred men who composed the entire company, there were two pieces of horse artillery; but in the effort to force these guns through a dense intervening wood, one of them became completely disabled. The other, while the hour was still dark, was brought up to the top of a hill which overlooked the turnpike and the procession of wagons.

All the rangers had now been concentrated and were eager and ready for the attack. No hesitation to undertake it was felt, although there were at least two thousand Federal soldiers to be faced and defeated if the work of destruction and capture was to be thorough. As they stood at attention in the faint light of dawn, the first sign, apart from the rumble of wheels, which they had of the wagon train was the vast cloud of dust floating up from the highway, over which many hundreds of animals were slowly tramping. With the increasing light, they could see the plain below them more and more clearly, until they gradually distinguished, one after another, the canvas-topped army wagons, with their teams and drivers.

At the word from Mosby, the cannoneers of the sound gun fired off a twelve pound shot, but the range was too high, and the ball passed over the train.

A second shell quickly followed. This was more successful and struck one of the wagons. The sound of the first shell and the explosion of the second in their midst, being entirely unexpected, and the roar reverberating loudly among the hills at that quiet hour, created at once a scene of the wildest alarm and confusion; and before the commotion could subside, a third shot was discharged in the midst of the wagons.

Instead of halting to find out whether resistance was practicable, the guards endeavored to hasten the retreat of the whole

The frenzied drivers cracked their whips and shouted

train as giving more promise of escape. The frenzied drivers cracked their whips and shouted at their mules; the drovers frantically belabored the horses and cattle in order to urge them forward at the top of their speed; while the crowd of hangers-on took to their heels, in a wild effort to reach the head of the train.

Encouraged by the spectacle of this helpless tumult, and fearing lest their prey might get away after all, the whole body of rangers, three hundred strong, galloped down from their position on the neighboring ridge, and yelling and firing off their revolvers as they advanced, were quickly up to the very line of the turnpike. As they drew near, the confusion there only increased. The drivers, in their deadly anxiety to escape from the shots of the troopers, now coming right on them, attempted to pass each other, and, in doing so, ran their wagons together, knocking off bodies and wheels alike; the infantrymen, lost in the terrifying jam, could make no stand; while the cavalrymen were engaged in riding wildly backwards and forwards in their attempt to restore order in the disorganized train. But this was impossible at first in the midst of all that deafening noise caused by the braying of mules, the lowing of cattle, the neighing of horses, the shouting of drivers, the cries of the camp followers, the crack of rifles and revolvers, and the triumphant yells of the rangers.

Just when the stampede seemed about to end in the complete self-destruction of the wagon train, and the dispersion of the drove of horses and mules and the herd of cattle, the Federal officers were able to bring to bear some organized resistance with the soldiers whom they had succeeded in concentrating. Squads of these posted themselves behind the stone fences and bravely fought until compelled to retire by a determined charge. This intermittent fighting went on along the turnpike for at least a mile and a half and aided many of the wagons to escape.

Ceasing the pursuit, the rangers went back to find out what proportion of the train had fallen into their hands. Knowing that they had only a short time to complete the work of destruction before the enemy would return in force, they started in at once to unhitch all the teams left behind and to rifle the loads; and when this was finished, they set fire to the wagons and their contents whenever of a kind that was too heavy to be taken away. A safe in which one hundred thousand dollars in greenbacks had been placed was overlooked and thus escaped seizure.

It was now eight o'clock in the morning, and the rangers were ready to leave the ground. Mosby had decided to return at once to the country east of the Blue Ridge, from which he had come the previous day; but how was he, with the small force under his command, to carry off three hundred prisoners, nine hundred head of live stock, and a large quantity of portable booty of all sorts? There were at least twenty-five miles to be traversed before he could reach headquarters in Fauquier county; and the chain of the Blue Ridge had to be passed before the journey was over. Moreover, not only the sound piece of artillery, which had done such execution, was to be taken back, but also the piece which had been disabled before the fight began.

"What are you going to do with that broken gun?" Mosby asked of the cannoneers.

"We are going to take it back home on the other gun," was the reply.

The mules, horses, and cattle were run together in a single drove; the captives were collected in one body; the rangers took the positions assigned them; the order to march was given, and the strange procession started upon the journey that was to end beyond the mountains. Among the articles which had been dragged out of the wagons before they were burnt were numerous Federal uniforms. The insides of these were turned outside in order to expose the red, white, and black of the linings, and in that reversed parti-colored shape, were worn by many of the men for the purpose of exciting the derisive amusement of their companions.

A large number of musical instruments of different kinds had also been captured, and the whole air was alive with the strains in all keys – some perfectly harmonious, others exactly the opposite – which were produced by the soldiers in playing on them. The horses and mules, running loose, were adding to the noise by their neighing, braying, and kicking; and the several hundred head of cattle further increased the pandemonium by their wild bellowing, and by rolling in the dust of the highway under the very feet of the rangers.

When the entire body of men and animals reached the banks of the Shenandoah, they plunged in pell mell, and while many of them were swept down stream by the current, all in the end got safely to the eastern side and resumed the journey. By four o'clock in the afternoon, they had passed the mountains and were descending the eastern slope.

As soon as the rangers halted for the night, they counted the livestock, which they had now succeeded in driving to a place beyond all danger of capture; they found that they had in their possession six hundred horses and mules, and two hundred and fifty cows and bullocks. About fifty head of all kinds had strayed and been lost on the road. The horses and mules were soon divided among the troopers; the cattle were corralled to be sent off next day to General Lee's army; and a squad was appointed to take the prisoners far within the Confederate lines. About one hundred wagons had been destroyed by fire before the rangers left the turnpike, and a great quantity of stores of all sorts consumed. The entire loss of Mosby's command amounted to only two men killed and two wounded.

Emboldened by the success of this sensational raid, Mosby, in October of the same year, determined to repeat it. He struck the Baltimore and Ohio railroad, the chief artery of supply for the Federal army in the Valley, at a point not far from Harper's Ferry. He had learned through his scouts on the day this occurred that a train was expected at a certain hour over the railway which would be conveying several hundred thousand dollars to be used in paying off the Federal soldiers posted in that region. It would be easy enough to throw the cars off the track simply by ripping up the rails at a curve which would shut the engineer off from a long view of the roadbed ahead of him; but Mosby was anxious to prevent a complete smash-up, as this would endanger the lives of the numerous civilians who were certain to be on board. How was such an extreme catastrophe to be avoided? By taking the rails up at a spot where there was no embankment, and where the cars would be thrown against the side of a cut. Was it possible to find a curve in a deep cut, for this only would afford the precise condition that he considered necessary for the accomplishment of his purpose?

After exploring the line for some distance, he came upon a piece of track that fulfilled all his requirements. The horses were hidden away behind the leaves of the nearest brushwood, while the men lay down just far enough beyond the edge of the cut to conceal their bodies, and yet close enough to keep them in earshot of the faintest echo that would indicate the approach of the treasure train.

The night was so cold that they found it difficult to get rid of the chill, for no fires were permitted to be lighted, and Mosby would not tolerate the use of stimulants; indeed, he never allowed his followers to drink either on the march or in bivouac, although the scene of their operations, not only now, but from the beginning, had lain in a country where illicit distilling was one of the principal occupations of the mountaineers, and where liquor was always to be obtained at an excessively low price.

The troopers, huddled together high above the cut, were too much engaged in listening for the sound of the expected train to feel drowsy or fatigued, or to trouble long about the coldness of the air. At midnight, the clatter of the cars, still several miles away, was faintly distinguishable, and every minute caused the sound to increase in volume, until at last it seemed to be only a few hundred yards away. The whole night soon vibrated to the roar of the wheels and the puffing of the engine.

The rangers, knowing the fate that would almost immediately overtake the train, held their breath in suspense; and their sense of excitement was not diminished by the thought that the treasure on board was certain to be guarded by many Federal soldiers, who would not allow it to be carried off without a fight. They leaned towards the edge of the cut as far as they dared to do in their fear of becoming visible in the light of the engine rounding the curve. Suddenly, the head lamp flashed full in their eyes; the train rushed around the corner; and in a moment, the engine, reaching the part of the roadbed from which the rails had been torn away, ploughed up the ground for many yards, and finally, amidst the roar of escaping steam, the grinding of the numerous coaches, and the outcries of the passengers, rolled helplessly into the ditch, a great mass of hot broken iron buried deep in the hissing mud.

The rangers hardly waited for the catastrophe to be completed before they leaped, revolvers in hand, down the steep slope of the cut, and rushed to the side of the derailed cars. The conductor, who seemed to have understood at once the cause of the disaster, appeared at the door of a coach which had not left the track, with a lighted lantern in his hand, and as he waved it backward and forward, he cried out, "All right. Gentlemen, the train is yours."

Several of the rangers quickly mounted the steps of the first car, and on pushing through the door found it partly occupied by immigrants from Europe, who were unable to speak the English language; but there were other passengers who could, and some of these showed at once a disposition to resist the troopers. One man near the end of the coach raised his carbine to shoot at them, but before he could fire, he was struck by the bullets from their revolvers; and this decisive action immediately cowed the rest of the company.

The rangers soon noticed that two officers were very solicitious for the security of a large bag and box which they had in their possession; this excited their suspicion; and when these receptacles were examined, it was found that they were crammed to the brim with newly printed greenbacks. Bag and box were turned over promptly to Mosby as containing the treasure which he had been expecting, and he at once instructed two of his most trusted men to take possession of them, and having mounted their horses, to carry the money off to a spot in the Blue Ridge where it would be kept in safety until the whole band should return from the raid.

The train was composed of ten cars altogether, and in addition to the immigrants and the officers, was conveying a large number of civilians and soldiers. The coaches, as soon as they had been thoroughly explored, were set on fire. All the soldiers, who had made no resistance, were placed under guard with a view to their being marched away to the east of the mountains. Among them was an Austrian who had received a commission in the Federal Army. His ring had been taken as a part of the booty by one of the troopers, and its loss had thrown him in a state of great agitation. In broken English, he earnestly begged to be brought before Mosby, and when his request was complied with, he told the Partisan Leader in excited tones, which still further confused his speech, that the ring was an heirloom and could not be replaced; and he pleaded that it might be at once returned.

Mosby coldly scrutinized the Austrian's new Federal uniform before he replied. He then burst out, "What the devil did you want to come over here to fight us for?"

"I came to learn de tactics."

Mosby's stern face relaxed.

"The loss of the ring is a part of the learning, perhaps," he said, with a repressed twinkle of his eye.

But he ordered that the ring should be returned, and at the same time he warned the foreigner that he must, in the future, rely upon himself for the retention of his own property. He was presented with a considerable amount of Confederate money, which he was told would be of more use to him in Libby Prison than Federal greenbacks.

The captives, having been brought together in one body, were marched rapidly away under the escort of the rangers, and, without casualty, were delivered the next day to the Confederate authorities. The men who had been entrusted with the custody of the greenbacks reached the appointed place in safety; and when the bag and box were afterwards opened in the presence of Mosby and the whole band, they were found to contain one hundred and seventy thousand dollars. In the division of this sum, which immediately followed, each ranger received twenty-one hundred dollars as his share. It was Mosby's rule to retain no part of the booty of a raid as his portion, and he did not break that rule in this instance. He always paid for his horses and their equipment with his private means, a fact that strengthened his influence with his men by proving his willingness to sacrifice his own interests to enhance their profits from each expedition.

The exploit of capturing the train and the money bag and box of the two Federal paymasters created a panic among the other paymasters in the Federal service who happened to be stationed in that part of the theatre of war.

"I have my funds in the parlor of the United States Hotel," telegraphed Paymaster Ladd to headquarters at Washington. "They are now guarded by a regiment. I shall make no move until I can do so safely; and in the meantime, I await your orders."

There was a large body of troops posted at Wheeling at the time of Mosby's raid on the railway. They were concentrated there previous to their removal to Washington, but instead of their being transported by the straight line directly through Harper's Ferry, as had been intended, they were conveyed to the Capital by a very circuitous route to avoid the possibility of a catastrophe to their train by a dash of the rangers.

The Federal military authorities made at once an almost frantic effort to capture the bold raiders and their leader; troops were dispatched, in feverish haste, to every point of the compass in that region of country; and there were many conflicting and confusing movements on their part, but all in vain. As one of the rangers himself has recorded, while all this commotion was at its height, a memorable scene was occurring in a little village in Loudon county: "There, undisturbed by any fear of interruption, great sums in crisp greenbacks were handed around equally and liberally among eighty of Mosby's grateful and admiring followers. The incident was closed."

CHAPTER ELEVEN
Private Munson's Escape From Prison

☆   ☆   ☆   ☆

On one occasion, Mosby was informed that a detachment of Federal cavalry was engaged in a short raid from a camp which they had established in sight of the Blue Ridge, and not far from the principal haunts of the Partisan Leader and his rangers. He at once sent off Captain Franklin with a picked body of men, including private Munson, who was a mere boy in years, to check their advance. They soon came upon the Federal troopers occupying a naturally strong position, and drawn up in bristling array to receive their onset. Franklin thought that, if he should attack them simultaneously in front and in rear, they could be quickly compelled to retire from the spot as untenable; but before the flanking party could make the necessary detour, the frontal assault had been beaten off; and when the assault on the wings took place, it was met by the concentrated fire of the entire Federal force.

The Confederates had marched forward in ranks of fours in delivering the flanking attack; and in the very first rank was private Munson. Before he was aware of it, he was left alone by the retreat of his comrades after their recoil before the sudden storm of bullets. His first impulse was to rush headlong against the line of Federal troopers opposite him, in the hope of breaking through by the impact, and escaping to the fields beyond; but even his eye, that rarely shrank from the prospect of the rashest enterprises, perceived at a glance that he must inevitably be shot down as he careered toward the enemy in the very muzzles of hundreds of pistols and carbines.

He quickly turned the head of his horse and galloped off in the opposite direction, followed by a fusillade of bullets. Unfortunately for him, a stone wall stood in his way. He rode at it not doubting that the mare would take it without the smallest hesitation; but on coming up to it, she suddenly balked, and neither whip nor spur, vehemently applied, could make her rise to the necessary leap.

Munson jumped down from the saddle, scrambled over the wall, and fled at the top of his speed across the open fields to a large body of woods which he saw in the distance. In the meanwhile, the enemy were hot upon his tracks, and having discovered a gap in the wall, which enabled them to pass through without delay, soon came up with him and forced him to surrender. He was immediately stripped of his hat, plumes and gloves, pistols and belt, watch, and even his boots.

"The Yankees trimmed me well," he laughingly asserted in after times.

On the following day, he found himself on the train under guard on the way to Washington, where he was to be imprisoned. Among the soldiers entrusted with the custody of the numerous captives on board was a man who was indebted to him for many kindnesses while lying in the hands of the Confederates; and he not only recognized Munson as soon as he saw him, but also readily promised to assist him indirectly to escape by turning his eyes away, should the ranger steal from the train when it stopped at the next station to take on water for the engine. But before this station was reached, the guard was changed, and Munson decided it would be too risky to try to leave his car without collusion with the new man, who stood, with fixed bayonet, at the door.

Arriving in Washington, all the prisoners were first drawn up in the street, and then marched in one body towards the Old Capitol, now converted into a military jail. The ranger's plight was one of the worst of all among the captives; having been deprived of his outer clothes when seized, he had found a very poor substitute in an ill-fitting, cast-off suit which had been given him and that left him in a ragged and seedy condition. His feet were entirely naked of covering, for the pair of rough horsehide boots which he had received were several sizes too large for him to wear with comfort. But he was too accustomed to the importance of chance in the soldier's wild life to throw even these boots away; and he patiently bore them along over his shoulder in the hope that some one would interpret this action as a signal of distress, and either give him outright another pair or accept them in exchange.

Suddenly, another use for the heavy boots occurred to his ingenious mind; might it not be possible to swing them at the guard like a club? With the guard knocked unconscious to the ground by a blow from the boots, Munson might seize the opportunity to run up a dark alley and get safely away in spite of pursuit.

The man who walked next to him in the ranks had once been a resident of Washington, and was familiar with every street, however obscure, of the city. His name was Denis Darden. This man, being as eager to escape as Munson, received the whispered details of the latter's plan with warm encouragement and named the most convenient byway that might be used for their purpose. Before reaching it, they fell back from rank to rank, without attracting notice, until they had come to the last in the procession, which was followed by a single guard at each of its two corners.

Munson had taken the boots from his shoulders and was furtively experimenting as to the best manner of striking the nearest of the two guards with them, when some friends of Darden, who were looking on from the sidewalk, recognized him, and immediately ran out to greet him and to walk at his elbow some distance along the street. As they were still with him when the alley was reached, Darden leaned forward and whispered to Munson, that, should the two attempt to escape now, it would expose these friends to severe punishment, for it would certainly be taken for granted that they had been in collusion with the prisoners.

On arriving at the Old Capitol, Munson and Darden along with thirty-six other captives were shut up in a large room, the only window of which, by the irony of circumstance, faced the bronze statue of Liberty standing above the Halls of Congress. They afterwards had ample opportunity, from hour to hour, to inspect her graceful proportions and sadly to contrast the freedom which she suggested with their own shackled condition.

But Munson at least was not content with such reflections. His mind went to work at once revolving every possible chance of escape which his eye, roving inquiringly from side to side, could detect. It was, however, some days before any that arose appeared to him to offer the smallest prospect of realizing his hopes. But finally one did present itself. It seems that the privilege was allowed the group of captives to take an hour's exercise in the prison yard at night; Munson noticed that two negro scavengers were admitted at the same time; and he soon opened up a conversation with them while they were engaged with their work. It was with pleasure that he discovered that one of the men had formerly been the slave of a family in Virginia whom he numbered among his warmest friends; and this at once created a tie between them which he hoped might be used to assist him to escape.

Allowing some days to go by in order to make his proposition appear less abrupt, he, at the end of that time, quietly offered the negro five dollars in gold if he would permit him to take a seat in the garbage cart just before it should start for the outer gate that night.

"But, boss," replied the man, looking at him with alarm, "You's a white man, we's black."

Munson had not overlooked this fact; nor had he failed to think of the remedy for it.

"Leave that to me," said he quietly to his colored friend.

Retiring to the prisoner's room, he took a piece of burnt cork and blackened his face and hands so successfully that all trace of his real color was concealed. Drawing on his rough rawhide boots, and pulling his old hat down closely over his shock of hair, and rumpling up his shabby clothes still more, he soon joined the two negro scavengers in the yard.

"Whar's you bin?" said his new friend loudly and roughly, "you's bin loafin' sho'. Now take dis shovel and hustle. We's bin heah too long already."

Munson gripped the shovel and quickly surpassed his companions in the quantity of garbage which he threw into the cart. His vigor seemed to arouse their admiration, without, however, in the slightest degree exciting their emulation.

When the load had been completed, he took a seat beside his two companions in front of the cart, which was then started off for the outer gate. They got through the inner one without a challenge and drove up to the outer. The heavy iron barrier swung back and Munson could see the broad street and free sky line spreading away indefinitely. A heavy blow was given to the haunches of the cart horse and they moved forward to pass under the arch where the last sentinel was stationed; but in a minute, all the hopes of the prisoner were dashed – a bayonet was suddenly lowered and pointed straight at him. He could not fail to observe it or the stalwart figure in uniform which rose behind it. The brogue of the Irish voice which now spoke would have been sufficient in itself to stop him.

"Git down from that," it called out, "and go back to your quarters. Two of yez neegars come in and three of yez is thrying to go out."

The prisoner was compelled to return crestfallen to his room, but the Irish sentinel was too good natured to give information to the authorities of the supposed negro's attempt to escape. Munson was left at liberty to contrive some other scheme to elude his jailers. Noticing that a baker's wagon delivered a loaf of bread daily within the bounds, he approached the driver when no one was looking on and discovered him to be as susceptible to a bribe as the black scavenger. Having hidden himself under a mass of loaves, which had been reserved for another patron, he was soon delighted to find the wagon in motion on its way to the outer gate. On reaching the barrier, it came to a halt under the arch as usual before passing into the street. Munson could hear the heavy footfall and the rattle of the sentinel's accoutrements as he strode to the back of the vehicle to make his customary examination. In a twinkling, the ranger felt his foot seized in an iron grasp, and his whole body was quickly dragged out from under the loaves.

"The next time you thry to escape, young man," said the sentinel drily, "you had better hide your toes."

It was true. Not only the toes but the entire foot was exposed to sight at the back of the cart.

Again the sentinel was too amiable to report what was apparently a second prisoner's attempt to get away; had he done so, Munson would have been liable at the least to solitary confinement and at the most to the punishment of death. To neither penalty was he subjected because his frustrated efforts were not brought to the attention of the prison authorities.

But not all the sentinels were so considerate of the captives whose plans they were able to thwart. One of Munson's companions entered into a secret agreement with the soldier who stood guard under his window to allow him to pass after he lowered himself to the ground. Having succeeded in doing this by sawing through the iron bars and letting himself down by means of a rope which he had made out of the sheets and blankets of his bed, he received a bayonet thrust through the back as he started to steal away in the darkness.

Neither a terrible end like this, nor his own two failures could discourage the active brain and the determined spirit of the youthful ranger. He was too accustomed to peril to shrink long from any form of it, however imminent and alarming, and he was extremely restive under the restraints of his present situation. For the third time, he looked around him to find out whether there was not some new means which could be used to enable him to escape.

His inquiring eye had noticed that a hospital steward visited the prison at least three times each day, and that he wore on either arm a rather unusual insignia, consisting of a green strip at least two inches wide, with a narrower border of yellow braid. In the centre of this band, there was visible a figure of Mercury holding a staff encircled by the body of a snake and with spreading wings at the top. This design was also in yellow, and in sharp contrast with the green tint contiguous to it.

Would it be possible to impersonate the steward? To do so, it would be necessary first to procure garments which at least sufficiently resembled those the man wore to attract no notice from the casual eye. It happened that Munson had recently received from a wealthy aunt residing in New York a considerable sum in gold coin with which to supply his most urgent wants. He used a portion of this sum in buying the blue blouse of a bounty jumper whom he had found in the prison. His gray trousers, being still in sound condition, were accepted in a trade for a pair that would easily pass as blue in candle or gas light.

But how was he to obtain a substitute for the green strip and the yellow figure of Mercury which the steward wore on each arm?

Was it possible that the green strip could be cut from the linings of the gray jackets which his fellow Confederate prisoners still used? At night, when they were fast asleep, he took a knife and quietly ripped open these linings, one after another, in his search for what he needed, carefully sewing up each one before beginning on the next; but this trouble was taken in vain – there was not to be seen even one thread colored exactly as was required. Nor could he discover anywhere within the bounds of the prison a single object that would afford him that material. Green seemed to be the one tint which had been omitted from the colors of the different rooms and their contents.

During several days, he remained in a state of despair – the outlook for his escape seemed now to be entirely hopeless. Happening while in this mood to be lounging in the sutler's shop, he listlessly followed the motions of the man as he took down from the shelves box after box. Suddenly, Munson observed among these boxes, as they stood in a row on the counter, one that had a cover colored to the precise shade of greenness which he had been trying so hard to find. Suppressing his eagerness, he asked in an indifferent voice, "Will you let me have that green pasteboard box? I need something in which to keep my valuables."

The sutler laughed.

"Young man," he replied, "there are no burglars in this prison. Your valuables are perfectly safe in your pocket."

But, nevertheless, he very kindly and cordially made a present of the box as requested. Munson hurried away with it to his room, and at once, in the moonlight, began to cut the top in strips of the length desired. To his delighted astonishment, he soon discovered that the body of the box, though covered over with green, was really yellow strawboard beneath the first paper layer; and that, in dividing it up into strips, he had only to shave away this green edge to procure the yellow border which he needed for his insignia. Without any difficulty, he was thus able to manufacture the two bands which were to encircle his arms.

The Mercury, wand, and serpent required more ingenuity to reproduce them; but he finally succeeded in accomplishing it by cutting the joint figures in the green facing of the box and then peeling this away until he exposed the yellow paste-board beneath. It was then easy to repeat the several figures in this yellow material itself. They were not as delicately and artistically fashioned as if they had been of Florentine origin, but he trusted that their deficiencies would not be detected by the casual glances of the persons whom he would have to pass on his way to the prison gate.

Dawn was breaking when he finished his task. But before he retired to bed, he put on the blue blouse which he had bought – and also the pair of trousers which he had obtained by exchange, and having attached the insignia to the arms of the blouse, took as discriminating a look at himself as the gray light of dawn permitted. So soon as the opportunity offered, he spoke to Denis Darden of his intentions.

"You are a dead man if found out," said Darden in a warning voice. "The guards have orders to shoot the first man trying to escape; and even if you get out of the prison safely, it will be impossible for you to reach the other side of the Potomac."

But Munson was not to be persuaded to abandon his plan; and at last Darden fell in with it so far as to mention the names of several persons in Washington to whom he should apply for assistance, should he be able to get beyond the outer gate of the prison. That evening, just before the candles were lighted, the ranger put on the blouse and trousers; and having covered up these garments and the insignia on his arms by donning an over-coat lent him by one of his companions, he went out into the prison yard, accompanied by Darden, as if both intended to take the exercise permitted at that hour. The sentinel, thinking that this was their purpose as usual, allowed them to pass without a chal-lenge. On reaching the dark shadow of the wall in the yard, Munson pulled off the overcoat and handed it to Darden, who, having silently received it, turned away, overcome with emotion, to retrace his steps to the prison room.

Brave as Munson was, he afterwards acknowledged that he was fairly benumbed by his consciousness of uncertainty as he approached the door of the long hall through which he had to pass before he could reach the prison gate. As he entered, the sentinel glanced at him a second and then turned his eyes away with indif-ference. Encouraged by this unsuspicious reception, the ranger threw out his breast, and so held off his arms that the insignia came into conspicuous view as he moved down the crowded apartment on his way to the further door. No one stopped or spoke to him; it was simply taken for granted by those who knew the hospital steward personally that this new man was acting as his substitute, either on this single occasion or for several days, while his superior was enjoying a short holiday. The inner guards bowed respectfully as he went by and bade him good night; and he made his way with equal ease through the group of the relief force which was just about to come on to take their place. He was now approaching the precincts of the outer gate, where he had been stopped twice when on the very eve of escape and ignominiously sent back to his former bounds. It seemed to him that he could already feel the fresh air from the open world outside blowing against his cheek; that he could see the lamps shining from the tops of their posts; and hear the noise of hurrying feet, and rolling wheels, and all the other varied sounds that echo along the streets. Would he be again halted when he had only one step to take to win

win his old liberty of life?

Whatever apprehension he might have felt at the moment, there was no indication of fear or uncertainty in his bearing as he came in sight of the guard who was charged with opening and closing the street gate. This man did not recognize him or glance at him with suspicion; slipping the bolt back and bowing politely to the disguised prisoner, he allowed him to pass out without one word except a friendly "Good night, Sir," which was repeated by the sentinel standing under the outer arch. The bolt clicked sharply behind Munson and he was once more a free man in the world at large.

But where was he to go? There could not have been for him a more dangerous place than this city through which he was now called upon to thread his way if he was to escape to the hills beyond the Potomac. It was full of soldiers and persons in the civil service of the Government, all of whom were enemies so unrelenting that, if they were to meet him on the street and should see into his real character, they would have him arrested on the spot.

How was he to find his way to the houses of the people who had been recommended by Darden as certain to give him an asylum? He was without any knowledge at all of the streets of Washington, and he ran a serious risk, should he inquire of the foot passengers whom he should encounter, for this would indicate at once that he was a stranger in town at a time when all strangers in the capital were looked upon with suspicion. But there was no other course for him to pursue. Tearing the insignia from his arms, which he had forgotten to do while meditating, he started off in the direction in which he supposed the boarding house kept by the lady whom Darden knew as a Southern sympathizer was situated. In asking the way, he was prudent enough to mention only the number of the house. On reaching it, and ringing the bell, he was met at the door by a negro servant.

"I don't reckon you kin see de Missis at dis' hour," he said, looking the ranger over from head to foot very superciliously. "Your name, sah, if you please."

In a short time, the lady appeared. Munson whispered in

her ear.

"Never heard of you," she answered in a tone of agitation. "George," she said, sharply turning to the servant, "go up stairs and shut that window."

When the negro had reluctantly disappeared, the lady drew Munson into the hall.

"Do you want money?" she asked hastily, and before she could receive a reply, had pressed a roll of greenbacks into his hand; but he quickly returned them.

"No, I only wish you to conceal me for a day or two, or at least for the night."

"Impossible. I am suspected as a Southern spy, and this house will be the fu'st place searched when your escape is known."

She then gave him the name of a Southern sympathizer who would probably afford him a hiding place until he could leave the city with safety. Catching the footfall of the servant coming down the stairway, she pretended to shuffle Munson unceremoniously out of the doorway, and as he descended the steps, he heard her scolding the negro and threatening to dismiss him if he admitted another tramp to the house.

It was not until the ranger had visited at least four other houses, and been turned away with the same anxiety and agitation from all, that he at last received a cordial invitation to remain from the warm-hearted mother and sister of Denis Darden; but he knew that their house would be among the very first to be ransacked for his capture. By this time, the roll had been called at the prison and his absence discovered. Already the pursuers must be out on the streets and going through suspected residences in the hope of catching him before he could cross the Potomac.

He had now but one more number to look up, and should the people there turn their backs on him, he would be left without any possible refuge. As he made his way thither by the directions which Mrs. Darden had given, he kept to the darkest streets and alleys, and avoided passing through groups of people who might scrutinize him too curiously. The house which he was endeavoring to find was the "palace" of a gambler named Lunsford, which was one of the most notorious resorts of the capital, and at night was haunted by many dissipated military officers and civil officials. He loitered in the neighborhood until midnight and then boldly entered. A miscellaneous crowd of men was present, among whom he noticed many Federal uniforms, which made his own blue blouse less conspicuous. Lunsford having been pointed out to him, he went straight up to the gambler, and in a whisper, informed him of his predicament.

"Turned away five times!" exclaimed Lunsford in low tones. "Served you right. Why did you not come to me first? Denis must have told you that I could be trusted. Confound you, the delay may cost you your liberty. Now go right in that back room and get some grub, and prepare to light out from Washington before daybreak."

As soon as Munson had swallowed his supper, the gambler put his manager in charge of the establishment for the rest of the night and started with the ranger for Georgetown.

"Let us get away as quietly as we can," he said. "Some of those soldiers in the room next to ours were sent there to look out for you."

It was two o'clock in the morning when they drew up at a small hotel in Georgetown which was under the management of a Frenchman. Thrusting a roll of bills into Munson's hands and directing his host to keep him in hiding until he could provide a safe escort across the river, the generous and kind-hearted gambler jumped into his buggy and returned at once to Washington.

It was a difficult undertaking to find a person not likely to excite the suspicions of the sentinels who would have to be passed along the road to the bridge. But finally, an arrangement was made with a countryman who visited the city daily to sell the produce of his market garden; and even in his case it was not until his wavering purpose had been braced by the gift of a bottle of brandy that he consented to run so serious a risk to his own liberty. It was first decided that Munson should pose as the old man's son; and the two then mounted the cart and set out. It was not until the last picket was reached that any delay in their progress occurred.

"Where did you get that boy from, farmer?" he asked suspiciously, when he had ordered the cart to be stopped. "He was not with you when you passed here this morning."

The old fellow swore loudly to the contrary; but the picket continued for some time to look incredulously at Munson. Finally, he grew friendly and asked for a drink.

"I am a temperance man," replied the market gardener, "I never took a drop in my life."

In the end, they were permitted to go on.

As soon as the picket was lost to sight by a turn in the road, the old man very cautiously drew the brandy bottle from his pocket.

"Sonny," he said, with a wink at Munson, after he had swallowed a long draught, "if you was as badly scared as I was just now, you'd be mighty glad to take a swig out of this bottle, young as yer is."

There were two important difficulties which the ranger, after parting with the market gardener, had to overcome if he was to succeed in returning to his command – he had to avoid all pickets and straggling troopers; and he had also to obtain food along the road from day to day.

Pursuing the safest route, he went back across the Potomac after arriving at a point opposite Montgomery county in Maryland. As he was tramping along, tired in body and very unkempt in appearance, he overtook a Federal rural guard, who was making his daily round on horseback. They at once fell into conversation, in the course of which the man gave him a friendly warning.

"Be careful, my boy," he said, "to keep away from the river. The pickets might take you for a rebel and shoot you. Suppose you let me show you the right way for you to go. I can accompany you some distance."

The ground on either side of the road was covered with a thick mantle of snow, and the roadbed itself was very slippery from a coating of ice. Munson, every now and then, would lose his footing, and he only prevented himself from falling by grasping the neck of the horse or the trooper's leg or saddle. In doing this, in one instance, his hand struck the guard's holster; immediately the thought flashed through his mind: why not grab the pistol, shoot the man, and take possession of his carbine, horse, and warm coat? He would, with such an equipment, find no difficulty in escaping quietly from the hostile region through which he was traveling so slowly and so laboriously. It was now night, but he could easily see, in the light of the moon, the weapon swung at the guard's back, which would have assured him protection from recapture even if he were detained in that dangerous country for some time by the risk of running upon the pickets along the river.

As they moved on, Munson noticed that the trooper's foot had slipped from the stirrup. A sudden and vigorous pull by the ankle, and the horseman might be drawn in a struggling heap to the ground and dispatched. There was a large tree just ahead, and in its deep shadow the first grasp might be taken before the man would have the smallest suspicion of his intention.

The ranger had fully resolved to venture it, when the trooper, observing his silence, leaned over from his horse and said in a very kindly voice, "If you are tired, comrade, I will walk and let you ride a spell. I guess it must be pretty toilsome jogging along these frozen roads."

At once, all thought of harming the man vanished from Munson's mind; and when they parted, they shook hands with the warmth and sympathy of a friendship that had been tested by an equal share in the hard conditions of war. The trooper never knew that he had, on that occasion, looked squarely in the face of Death for several minutes; and that his own kindly spirit alone had saved him from the fatal blow.

On approaching the banks of the Potomac, Munson directed his steps towards the home of a Southern sympathizer, who had been recommended to him by his host in Georgetown. Here he was received with warm hospitality, and was generously provided with an abundance of thick clothing to keep out the chill of the biting weather when he should continue his journey into Virginia.

The second night, he set out for the Potomac, but before reaching it was compelled to hide himself behind a high rock to avoid being seen by two Federal pickets who happened to be passing. Leaving his place of concealment when the voices had died away, he walked down cautiously to the riverside to find that the thaw which had begun that morning had so far weakened the ice still covering the surface that he could hear it crackling and growling as if it were about to break up. But it was now too late to hesitate. He started out to cross over, and as he gingerly went along, the sheet beneath his feet would hum and warp to such a degree that he was apprehensive less he should sink into the running water at the next step. At one point, he slipped and fell, but the ice there was strong enough to bear the weight of the blow, and he picked himself up and set out again for the Virginia side.

To add to the risk of the passage, he could see the fires of the Federal pickets shining here and there along either shore; and he had reason to fear that his figure, outlined against the night sky as he advanced, might have been observed and steps taken to intercept him so soon as he should reach the bank. But on leaving the ice, he met no guard to challenge and stop him. and he silently took refuge in the nearest wood under the screen of darkness.

On the journey to Leesburg, he was forced to conceal himself from time to time in thick bushes to escape the eyes of Federal raiders; and the house in the town where he passed a night was subjected to a search while he was hidden in one of the closets.

On joining Mosby at Upperville, his first inquiry was about the fate of the mare which had thrown him into the hands of the enemy by balking at the stone wall. He was told, to his delight, that she had followed in the track of the flying troopers and had been caught and led in by one of his comrades. When he visited the stable where she was kept, the mare recognized him at once and showed her pleasure at the sight of him by a loud whinny. He threw his arms around her neck, and was not afterwards ashamed to admit, that, in his relief, he had given away to a hearty cry.

CHAPTER TWELVE
Adventures of a Scout

☆ ☆ ☆ ☆

The single purpose which every scout had in view was to collect information for the guidance of his superior officer. He was sometimes accompanied by several comrades, but, as a rule, he preferred to wander about alone, either on foot or on horseback; relying upon no arm but his own; trusting to no weapons but his revolver and his sabre; and leaving it to no mind and no eye to direct his footsteps except those with which nature had endowed him. He always felt indifference to or contempt for danger, since danger was the only atmosphere which he breathed; and his thirst for adventure was unquenchable, although every hour of his life was crowded with reckless exploits and hair-breadth escapes.

The scout was always a man who appeared to have been born for his perilous calling; he took it up, not with the hope of promotion, or even with a desire to fulfill a sense of duty, but rather in the spirit which can find no satisfaction in existence unless it is keyed up to the highest pitch, like the life of the roving knight-at-arms in the Age of Chivalry.

He advanced and retreated; he made his way to this region or to that; he bivouacked or moved on just as his own judgment dictated at the moment. He haunted the woods and the brakes like the sylvan gods of antiquity, who drew a contented breath only in the shade of the trees. His step was as soft and noiseless as the footfall of a faun or a hare; his eye as keen in its glance and as unceasingly watchful as the eye of a furtive lynx that had been able to preserve its life only by sleepless vigilance; his tongue as silent as that of the cunning fox stalking its prey. He never lay down in his blanket under the screen of the densest copse of pine or scrub oak to snatch a short sleep that he did not keep one ear open for the crackling of a twig or the echo of a far-away shot.

There was not a hog-path in the forest, not a deer-walk running down to some shady stream, not a woodchopper's road winding aimlessly about through the dark underbrush, that he did not know by the yard and by the mile. During night and day, he prowled like an invisible ghost around the enemy's camps, peeping warily out from behind a bush or rock, without ever showing his face or using his voice even in a whispered exclamation to himself, and with his whole being concentrated in his eyes.

All this time, his horse was tethered somewhere deep in the forest, where it patiently waited for the return of his prying master.

Should the enemy come suddenly and unexpectedly upon him, which rarely happened, and he fell, then his body lay where it dropped, and there were no soldier's hands to gather up his bones from the bleaching wind and sunshine. He died alone as he had lived. He had been a solitary rover, and his fate remained a mystery like the exploits of his secretive career.

If, on the other hand, he survived the encounters which he could not always avoid, however great his caution and his prudence, then he returned to the headquarters of his commanding officer without looking upon the facts accompanying his escape as of sufficient importance or novelty to be related to his comrades. Was not dangerous adventure the routine of his existence? Why should he talk of that which was so constant and so habitual? He simply took it all for granted, and rarely spoke, even with the most modest words, of the perilous scenes through which he had passed, or of the risks which he had been compelled to run at every hour of his wanderings.

Such was the type to which the flower of Confederate

scouts, Frank Stringfellow, belonged. No hero in the pages of Scott, Stevenson, or Dumas ever found himself in more hazardous situations, as imagined by those authors, than this young Virginian did in reality in the course of the Civil War. Two of his adventures, picked out of the great number that might be selected, are of particular interest.

In November, 1863, Meade lay encamped in the neighborhood of Culpeper Court-House. Large bodies of Federal troops were stationed at different points, but so near together that they could be further concentrated for attack, if desired, within a very short time. What were the designs of the Federal General as revealed by his movements? That was a question which General Lee wished to have answered, and as the first step towards obtaining the information wanted, Stringfellow, accompanied by two comrades, was sent out to prowl around the Federal posts and to discover what should appear to be the enemy's immediate intentions.

The three men, mounted on spirited and well-trained horses, made straight for one of the largest of the Federal camps. Some time before they came in sight of it, they leaped from their saddles, tied their horses in a covert, and stole cautiously through the underbrush towards the quarter from which sounds of the presence of troops came. At last a small opening in the trees revealed to them the spectacle of an encampment which appeared to cover many acres with the white canvas tops of its tents. A closer view brought out all the usual features of such a station – the sentinels pacing their several beats; the soldiers lounging singly or in groups around their separate areas; the officers passing to and fro or engaged in conversation with each other.

Throughout the day, Stringfellow and his companions, quietly and without being observed, circled about the spot with the purpose of calculating as far as practicable the number of men embraced in the assemblage before them. Towards night, they retired to a place lying some distance back, in the hope that they would be able to encounter here stragglers, who might be captured without alarming their comrades. It was from such stragglers that they were certain to obtain information which would confirm or disprove the correctness of their impressions of what they had already seen. Foragers were always abroad in the vicinity of so large a camp, and it was possible that they might be easily seized and held, as they were often simply the unarmed hangers-on of the sutler's department.

The three scouts had been moving about so energetically for many hours that they decided that they would lie down for a short rest; and they chose, with that view, a spot which was completely encircled by a dense growth of trees. It was now night, and the air had grown so damp and so cold that they determined to light a fire, which they thought would be fully screened from sight without. Their fatigue and the grateful warmth combined made them drowsy at once, and not many minutes had passed before the three were fast asleep wrapped in their blankets. So sound was their slumber that they were not awakened by a rain which set in, and they continued to lie just as they had thrown themselves down on the ground until day had dawned. At that early hour, a squad of six Federal infantrymen set out from camp to scour the country for butter, eggs, and poultry, and on their way, they stumbled upon the hiding place of the three Confederates. Stringfellow was awakened by a hand removing his blanket, which he had drawn over his face.

"How are you, Johnny Reb," exclaimed a derisive voice. "Come get up. These wet quarters are not comfortable enough for you. We can do a great deal better than this for you in the camp."

Stringfellow blinked as if he were still half asleep, but he was taking in, with the rapidity of lightning and the furtiveness of a hunted catamount, the figures before him and weighing the chances of escaping. He had resolved that he would not surrender. His companions had not been aroused, and if he had to act quickly, no reliance was to be placed on their assistance. Closing his eyes and drawing his blanket more closely about his form, he turned over as if to resume his interrupted slumber.

"Go away," he muttered drowsily, "I want to sleep."

The Federal soldiers laughed immoderately at this speech, and before they could recover their gravity, the scout had reached down to his belt and laid his fingers on the hilt of his pistol. As he did so, he drew a long breath and pulled the blanket further up over his head in order to conceal the movement of his free hand. By a second movement, he drew the pistol from its holster and quietly cocked it.

Hardly had this been done when the leader of the Federal squad grasped the blanket and roughly dragged it away. Immediately, a shot rang out, and he fell dead across the body of the prone scout; a fact that saved the latter, for the other Federals, in their astonishment, fired off their revolvers so confusedly that only the corpse of their comrade was struck. As Stringfellow leaped to his feet, he discharged his pistol at one of his assailants bringing him to his knees; and a shot at a second one was equally successful. The remaining men took to their heels. As the camp was very near, the scout was well aware that within a few minutes an entire company of pursuers would be hot on the trail of the three Confederates.

As soon as the Federal soldiers ran off, Stringfellow's two companions, without stopping to wait for him or to bring away their holsters and blankets, fled to the nearest forest, but with so little attention to each other's movements that they rushed off in different directions.

Before lying down to sleep the night before, Stringfellow had taken off his shoes, and he now found himself in his socks, which, however much it might at first quicken his flight, would soon expose his feet to sharp laceration, and thus in the end seriously impede his progress; but he had no time to think of this; and following the example of his companions, he made for the nearest covert as promising the earliest concealment.

In the meanwhile the enraged pursuers had started from the camp, and they had scattered at once so widely that, unless the scout could make his way towards the mountains, every avenue of escape would be closed; and even this avenue appeared a few minutes later to be shut when he saw a squad of cavalry galloping towards the foothills to cut him off from that asylum. He knew that he was now entirely surrounded and that nothing but the coolness of his own nerve and his skill in woodcraft could save him from capture; which he was fully aware would mean that he would be shot as a guerrilla; for while he still had on his Confederate uniform, a proof that he was not a spy, yet he had been in the immediate vicinity of the largest of the Federal camps, and had shot down a Federal soldier. He made up his mind that he would either get safely away or kill as many of the enemy as he could before he yielded up his own life. It was not the first time that he had been in imminent peril, and now, as formerly, he did not despair of escaping.

He quickly found himself in a large wood, and as he ran forward with bare head and shoeless feet, he could hear the enemy behind him and on either side shouting to each other, as they beat the covert, just as if he were some wild beast that could be forced out of his hiding place and shot as he leaped madly into view. Like a fox followed by a pack of hounds hot upon its scent, he turned, doubled, and circled, in the hope of throwing the pursuers off his track. He was soon driven out of that part of the wood where there was a heavy undergrowth, and unless he could get away from among the open trees, the trunks of which alone afforded him any cover, he would be seen, and either shot from a distance or run down and seized.

The edge of the forest was now only a few hundred feet away, and he descried in the open field which began at the end of this space a small clump of stunted pine; and for this refuge he made with all the speed of which he was capable. Leaping into the copse unobserved, he hid himself in the bushy top of a fallen tree and listened for the sounds of the approaching pursuers. If found, his fate would be hopeless, and in order to make the enemy pay dearly for his life, he reloaded his pistol and carefully inspected its caps; and when he saw that all was in perfect order, he placed himself in such a position that he could fire on the instant.

Hardly had he effected this, when four Federal soldiers left the wood and came straight towards the spot where he was concealed. Seemingly, they all passed by the clump of pines without stopping to make a search. Stringfellow, raising his head to ascer-

For this refuge he made with all speed.

tain whether this was so, caught the eye of one of them who had loitered behind the rest.

"Here he is, here he is," shouted the man to his companions, and numerous voices responded from every direction to the triumphant cry.

The scout leaped to his feet, pistol in hand, and for a moment he stood with his eyes fixed directly on the eyes of his nearest adversary; who appeared to be afraid to approach any closer until he could have the support of his comrades. The same feeling evidently governed the other three men when they had run back to the spot. Here was a desperate guerrilla to deal with, and they all silently decided that it would be best to await the arrival of the other soldiers, who were now seen rushing towards them through the wood. Already the scout was surrounded, and in a few minutes, the strength of the cordon would be increased an hundred fold.

"Oh, for a horse," was the thought that was uppermost in his mind as he gazed around at his enemies! His feet had been lacerated by stones and rough ground in the course of his flight, and he felt as if his ability to run further was almost spent. There seemed now at last to be left to him not the smallest avenue of escape.

He looked around with the gaze of sharp despair when he saw in the field not far off a young mule, which had been turned out without bridle or halter to crop the grass. With a jump forward and a loud shout, the scout made for the animal as fast as his legs could carry him. The suddenness of his action and the rapidity of his movements so confused the aim of his enemies that their fusillade of shots failed to strike him.

Mounting to the back of the mule at a bound, the scout dug his feet into its sides, and these blows, coupled with the fright which had been given it by the scout's wild leap, sent it galloping away, with its rider, hatless and shoeless, clinging with one hand to its mane, and with the other, grasping the butt of his pistol. Recovering from its astonishment after it had run for a considerable distance, the mule stopped and began to kick up its heels and to arch its back, in a determined effort to throw the scout; and as the latter had no means of keeping his very difficult seat, he very soon found himself lying flat on the ground; but in a twinkling, he arose to his feet, and followed by the shouts and shots of the enemy, who had again taken up the pursuit, he ran into a large body of woods that sprang up on the other side of the open field.

For some time, he fled through this forest at the top of his speed, but gradually his sense of fatigue grew overwhelming and he felt faint from his exertions. Now for the first moment too he became conscious of a burning thirst. His run fell off to a walk, and he looked about to find a stream or a spring, to which the character of the ground in sight appeared to be favorable. A few steps further brought him to the bank of a brook, in a narrow, grassy meadow, and he threw himself on his knees to drink of its cool waters.

Hardly had he quenched his thirst, when he heard again the calls and cries of his pursuers pushing straight towards him, and now at no great distance away. He felt that he did not have the strength to continue his flight, and that his capture was inevitable unless he could hide himself in the weeds that fringed the sides of the stream. He had barely taken refuge among them and drawn the stalks together about his prostrate body, when one of the enemy broke through the line of trees and came down the short slope to the margin of the rivulet. He walked backwards and forwards along the bank for a few feet with his eyes bent on the ground, and then suddenly called out to his comrades, who were now in earshot:

"Here are the prints of the guerrilla's knees in the sand. He ain't far off."

Soon all the members of the party had gathered on the spot and were eagerly studying the knee marks, and when satisfied by their scrutiny, they scattered to search for the fugitive, who, they were confident, was now almost again in their grasp. The little meadow contained several clusters of bushes, which seemed to offer a leafy nook of refuge; and these were in turn cautiously beaten and inspected.

All this time, the scout was lying on his back in the bower of weeds and grasses, with a cocked pistol in his hand and his ears acutely alert to the sounds and cries that accompanied the hunt. He had made up his mind, that, should his place of concealment be broken into, he would not attempt to get away. He was, in fact, now too exhausted to succeed in escaping by running off a second time. But before he should be shot down, he was determined to make the most of every load in his revolver.

All the rest of the meadow having been gone over minutely without success, the men were now slowly returning along the margin of the stream to the spot where they had detected the knee prints; and as they advanced, they were whipping and kicking up the adjacent growth of weeds and grasses and peering among the twigs of every branch.

In a few minutes, they had reached the place where the scout lay in hiding; and he could hear their oaths of disappointment uttered almost directly at his elbow. He grasped his cocked weapon more firmly, and as he did so, a hand was thrust forward to draw the curtain away; he could see the fingers that were about to expose his body; he gently raised the pistol sufficiently to get it in range to fire, and at once had the heart of his adversary practically at its muzzle; the next instant there would be an explosion, and several men were certain to fall before he himself should be killed. Then, as suddenly as it was advanced, the hand was taken away, and the tops of the weeds and grasses swung back to their natural position.

But was the scout saved? Might he not have been seen? And this withdrawal of the hand, might it not have been a ruse to secure first the cooperation of all the pursuers for the capture or destruction of the pursued? For a few minutes, he was in suspense in spite of the exclamations of chagrin and disgust which he overheard; and then the men began to disperse again in the continuation of their search.

Throughout the remainder of the afternoon, Stringfellow caught from his hiding place the distant cries and calls of his enemies. He did not venture to move until night had fallen. Passing the line of Federal pickets under the cover of darkness, he made his way back safely to the Confederate headquarters, which he reached at dawn.

It was in the course of the same year that a second incident occurred in the life of Stringfellow which brought him quite as near to a fatal ending of his career as the one already related. During the summer of 1863, large detachments of Federal troops were scouring all that region which lay just north of the upper tributaries of the Rappahannock. This country, as we have seen, was precisely suited to the furtive excursions of small partisan bands, and it was equally so to the secret operations of roving scouts. Stringfellow, by his boldness and success, was quite as well known to the Federals as Mosby himself, and it was with a feeling of great satisfaction that the information was received by a certain Colonel of Federal pickets that, at that very hour, he was unsuspiciously enjoying the hospitality of a family with Southern sympathies, whose home was situated not very far from camp.

The report was really true. The scout, knowing this family well, and anxious to obtain a brief rest and some diversion from the hard conditions of his calling, had gone to their house, indifferent to the risk of detection to which he was aware he would be exposed. It was not often that, in his hurried expeditions about the country, he had the opportunity of conversing at ease with these friends under their own roof and partaking of such an excellent supper as he was sure would be set before him in the well-remembered dining-room. He was unable to resist the temptation, and he boldly defied the dangers.

The meal was over and the scout was seated with the family, without a thought at the moment of taking either himself or his horse away from quarters of such unusual comfort and plenty; but even in that hour of social relaxation, he had not forgotten to keep his pistol ready to his hand in the belt around his waist. In the midst of the lively talk that was going on, his ears, ever alert to catch suspicious sounds, heard the clatter of approaching hoofs. He at once arose and cautiously went to the window to look out on the road. There he saw, as far as he could make out in the darkness, what appeared to be a large body of Federal cavalry, dispatched, he had no doubt, to apprehend him; and as the house would be at once encircled by the troopers, there seemed to be no hope of escape.

He had hardly turned away before a knocking at the door began and there was heard a loud cry for admission, mingled with the sound of the footsteps of the numerous cavalrymen who had dismounted in front of the building. Calmly telling his friends that he was surrounded, but that he intended to fight his way out, since a price had been set on his head by the enemy, he was about to make his way to the back door to carry out his purpose when the lady of the house hastily exclaimed, "Stop, stop, we can hide you in the garret." One member of the family ran to the window and called out "Who's there," while another rushed to the rear of the house and locked the back door. A third hurried the scout to the stairway that ascended from the hall. Before they could reach the second floor, a loud explosion shook the building – a dozen carbines had been fired at the front-door, and the balls had whistled about the ladies and buried themselves in the opposite wall. A resounding shout followed, and almost at once too the crash of shoulders thrown heavily against the door was heard.

But before an entrance could be thus forced, the scout and his companion had mounted to the garret. As the former looked around the empty apartment, with its bare, unplastered walls, he could not see a single nook or cranny where his body could be squeezed out of sight. There was no ceiling. Two beams ran across overhead, and resting on these were several wide planks not nailed down. The young lady pointed to them, and in a whisper, told him to raise himself up to one of them and to lie at full length on it. He quickly swung himself on high by leaping up and seizing the nearest beam; and having chosen the plank situated next to the eaves, lay flat down on it on his stomach.

The young lady, pausing only one moment to ascertain whether his body was entirely invisible to anyone looking up from below, and seeing that it was, quickly left the apparently unoccupied room and descended the stairs. Just as she reached the ground floor, the Federal troopers burst in the front door and poured into the narrow passage. The scout, prone on his plank in the dark garret, could hear every word spoken below.

"Madam," demanded the officer at the head of the troop, speaking to the lady of the house, "where has the guerrilla hidden himself? We have information that he is here."

"What guerrilla do you mean?" she inquired calmly.

"Stringfellow."

"Oh, he was here, but he went away some hours ago.

"That's not so," replied the officer angrily and threateningly. "You shall not trifle with me. The scoundrel is here this very moment. I shall have the house searched from top to bottom. Sergeant," he interrupted himself, turning to a non-commissioned officer at his elbow, "before we go any further, read the orders."

The sergeant, thus commanded, drew an official paper from his pocket and began to read its contents in a clear voice. Stringfellow and his outrageous exploits was the subject of the proclamation; he was described as a guerrilla, a bushwhacker, and a spy; no shrift whatever was to be shown him should he be overtaken; he was to be looked upon as an outlaw caught in the very act of committing a crime and to be sabred or pistoled on the spot without one moment's grace or the smallest atom of mercy. Death alone was to be his portion, death on the instant.

It was a terrific indictment which the scout overheard. A summary retribution, a lightning-like punishment, was all that he could expect should he fall into the power of the enemy. But his spirit was not cowed or his courage shaken by the words which the sergeant so distinctly recited; he felt for the pistols in his belt, which he kept always loaded and capped, and placing one on the plank in front of him, and holding on to the other, calmly awaited whatever fate should have in store for him.

He had fully mapped out in his own mind what he intended to do. It was not likely that more than two men would enter so small a room at once, as the presence of more would be certain to hamper their movements in an encounter. If his hiding place on the plank should happen to be discovered by these men, he had determined to fire first from above, and then to leap down, pistol in hand, and fire a second, a third, a fourth time, should it be necessary; and if either or both of the soldiers survived the shots, to endeavor, with all his might, to hurl him or them headlong down the stairway from the open door. There was a wooden projection just at this point, and here he would afterwards take his stand under cover and empty his revolver in the breast of whoever attempted to ascend the steps. Should he succeed in carrying out his plan so far, he was confident that the enemy could drive him from his position only in two ways – either by burning down the entire house, or by destroying it with the shells of their horse artillery.

So soon as the sergeant finished reading the proclamation, a minute search of the premises began. First, the ground floor was brought under a careful examination; dining-room, parlor, hall, kitchen, pantry – all were gone through, until not a corner, not a single foot of space in them had escaped the crutiny of the soldiers. Then the second floor, where there were numerous bedrooms, closets, and passages, was ransacked by them with even greater thoroughness, as if it were possible for a man to hide in a crevice with all the ease of a cricket, a cockroach, or a mouse. They got down on their knees and peered under the beds; they thrust their sabres through the sheets, blankets, and mattresses; they ran their cutlasses into the dresses hanging up in the wardrobes. Not one inch was left unexplored; but all to no purpose – the scout was not to be found. The men showed their disappointment by rough exclamations even in the presence of the women, who had been compelled to accompany them in order to hasten and make more easy the search.

Observing the narrow stairway that led up to the third floor of the house, the officer asked, in a very curt voice, of one of the young ladies, "Is there a room at the top?"

"Yes, a small garret."

"Will you show one of my soldiers the way? The guerrilla may be hiding there."

"Your man can ascend without me. The room is full of dust that will spoil my dress. I must decline to go."

The officer looked at her for a moment very suspiciously, then turned to a negro girl, one of the family servants, who had been carrying around a lighted candle while the search was going on, and said abruptly and authoritatively, "Come, show the soldier the way."

The girl laughed uneasily and seemed embarrassed.

"Lors, Marse Cap'en, dar's nubbody up dar sho'," she exclaimed.

"Obey my order," was the stern reply.

Drawing her dress about her ankles and holding the light high up, as if she were about to wade through a mass of contaminating mud and wished to pick her way as cautiously as possible, the girl very slowly and reluctantly ascended the stairway, followed by one of the soldiers carrying a cocked pistol in his hand.

The scout had heard from his plank under the eaves every word of this conversation with the officer, and was not surprised when his ear caught the sound of the mounting footfalls, and his eye saw through the open door the rays from the candle thrown on the railings of the stairway. The next minute, the girl reached the top of the steps and the dull, flickering, waving light penetrated to all parts of the garret, exposing to half view the bareness of the walls and the vacancy of the unswept floor, and causing the beams and planks to cast deep shadows. The young negress, pausing on the threshold, with the trooper just behind her, gave an exclamation of disgust, while she drew her skirts still more closely about her as if to save them from the taint of the accumulated dust.

"See dar," she said, "dar's nuttin' in dat room but dirt. I ain't gwine ter spile my dress in all dat dust, dat I ain't."

The man, with an oath, shoved her forward, and both entered the room. As the soldier peered curiously and not without apprehension around the apartment, Stringfellow, looking down with one eye through a small hole in the plank on which he lay, carefully measured his size and debated in his own mind whether it would be wisest to shoot him in the head or in the breast.

Discovery seemed to the scout to be inevitable. Here he

was only a few feet above the body of his adversary; so near, indeed, that he had to hold in his breathing to prevent its becoming
audible below. The slanting of the light, a scrutinizing look from
the farthest corner of the room, must divulge his presence. With
both pistols cocked and ready to hand, he awaited the moment of
detection. At the first exclamation from the trooper, he would fire
a bullet into his head, and leaping to the floor, roll the body down
the stairway and defy the whole troop of armed men to come up.

While this resolution was flashing through Stringfellow's
mind, the trooper, walking slowly around the room, was carefully
examining the walls and the corners, and here and there stamping
on the floor to test its solidity; nor did the smallest object escape
his examination, for he even prodded with his sabre the contents
of a box that he found leaning against one of the partitions. All
this while, the girl had been standing near the door muttering her
loathing for the dust and her fear of rats and mice.

Suddenly the man, disappointed in his inspection of the
floor and walls, turned his gaze towards the unceiled roofing, and
at once the girl moved forward and took position with the candle,
now burning low, directly under the plank on which Stringfellow
was lying. This action threw its shadow straight upward.

Could the scout's body be seen by the trooper? For a minute, the latter's eyes were fixed on the exact part of the plank
where lay the scout, who had put his finger on the trigger of his
pistol. Should he anticipate his enemy's shot and fire at once without waiting any longer? He had made up his mind to do this when
the trooper's intent gaze was withdrawn. The girl's ruse had
proved successful. Had the shadow of the plank been cast sideways against the roof, the outer line of its occupant's body would
have been seen by the soldier below, already suspicious of his
foe's presence; and a bullet would doubtless have followed immediately. With the shadow cast upward, the scout became invisible
from the same point of view, and the girl had possessed the wit to
anticipate this fact for his preservation. The man's repeated order
to her to move the candle this way or that way, as he peered upwards into every possible recess, did not influence her to alter the

slant of the shadow; and finally, fully satisfied that there was no one in the room but the candle bearer and himself, he turned towards the door to descend the stairs.

The scout drew a long breath of relief as he heard the footsteps of both passing down to the ground floor, where the officer and the rest of the troopers were waiting for the searcher's return. Keenly disappointed by his report, the officer sternly warned the lady of the house against offering Stringfellow any future entertainment.

"If the guerrilla is caught here," he said to her, "it will be necessary for me to turn your family out of doors. We will have to use the severest measures to prevent his friends from assisting him to our damage. He is one of our most dangerous enemies."

The officer soon mounted his horse, and accompanied by the entire troop, rode away at a gallop; but videttes had been left on the front road to guard the house. The scout, who descended when the sound of voices died out below, looking cautiously, with the members of the family, through a window, could see the uniformed figures in the darkness, ready to intercept him should it turn out that he had been hidden in the building after all. But he was not in the slightest degree disconcerted by the sight of them so far as his own chance of getting away was concerned; it, however, made it inadvisable for him to carry off his horse at that time, for to do so would inevitably expose his presence to the videttes; who, while they would be unable to capture him, would visit the penalty of his concealment and escape on the friends who had so courageously harbored and saved him by their fidelity and shrewdness.

He determined to leave the house on foot. Having bade a warm and grateful good-bye to his kind hostess and her family, he stole out of the rear door, and by creeping along under cover of the garden fence and afterwards keeping in the shade of a row of trees, he contrived with ease to reach the protection of a neighboring forest without having been challenged by the enemy. After an hour's tramp in the darkness, he found himself among the spurs of the Blue Ridge, and was soon enjoying the shelter of a home, the occupants of which were known to him as ardent sympathizers with the cause of the South.

CHAPTER THIRTEEN
The Cadets' Baptism of Fire

☆　　☆　　☆　　☆

The most famous military school in the South at the beginning of the war was the Virginia Military Institute, situated at Lexington, in the shadow of some of the loftiest peaks of the Blue Ridge. Here were trained many of the most distinguished officers of the Confederate armies. Throughout the great conflict, the cadets pursued their studies, but not infrequently, the sound of the guns broke in on the routine of their duties and aroused their gallant young souls to all the martial enthusiasm of veterans.

Down to the Battle of Newmarket, in the spring of 1864, where they received their baptism of fire, the battalion had not taken any part in a real fight, but they had been engaged in several unimportant military operations, such as the McDowell campaign in 1862, and the expeditions to drive off the raiding cavalrymen of Averill. If they were as yet ignorant of the sensation caused by the actual impact of musket balls and fragments of shrapnel, still they had been fully tested by the fatigue of long marches and by exposure to the roughest weather at all seasons. They too had bivouacked under the trees at night; had slept in their blankets; and had hungrily eaten food cooked at the camp fires. But none of them yet could point to the scars of wounds received in actual battle, or could drink to the memories of comrades who had fallen in the ranks at their side under the fusillades of the enemy. And until this, the true soldier's record in the field had been achieved, they refused to remain entirely satisfied with the peace of their barracks and recitation halls, although that peace might be varied at intervals by military tramps about the mountains in search of deserters or along the trail of retreating Federal troopers.

It was the experience of real warfare, with all its blood and glory, that they thirsted for; and so irresistible did this desire become, that, on one occasion, they assembled with great solemnity and drew up a formal resolution offering their services as a unit to General Lee.

Throughout the winter of 1863-64, they had found it especially difficult to restrain their martial spirit. The cavalry brigade of General Rosser, one of the most brilliant officers in this arm of the service, had been stationed in the vicinity of Lexington during that winter. His weatherbeaten and war-scarred veterans in uniform were to be seen at all hours about the grounds of the Institute, where they mingled with the admiring boys and stimulated their youthful ardor by tales of adventure on the march and in the charge. And this ardor had been further influenced by the gift of a flag, rent and blackened, which had been wrested from the standard bearer of the enemy in the midst of the foaming turmoil of battle.

The spirits of the young battalion were at once depressed and lifted up a short time later as they looked on the long procession of seasoned cavalrymen passing through the precincts of the Institute, on their return to the front, with their flags flying, and their pennons fluttering, in the mountain breeze and their sabres and accoutrements flashing in the sunlight. No wonder that some of the boys could not repress their warlike ambitions any longer, but must at once sever their connection with the place and follow in the track of the gallant cavaliers who had ridden away on that memorable morning. But it would not be long now before every member of the battalion would have an opportunity to receive that baptism of fire for which all appeared to be yearning.

In the spring of 1864, General Sigel was ordered by General Grant, who had taken personal command of the Federal armies in Virginia, to march up the Valley, and to hold it firmly as he proceeded, as the only means of preventing its further use as a granary by the Confederates. Sigel set his troops, twenty-five thousand in number, in motion on May 1st, with Staunton in view as his first important objective. The only force which could be brought forward promptly, in the hope of staying his progress, was a detachment of three thousand men under General Imboden.

The report spread that the Federals were steadily advancing, and the cadets, knowing that the Institute would certainly be invaded in the end, should Sigel not be stopped, became more eager than ever to take the field. At this time, the battalion consisted of two hundred and eighty boys, all of whom, with the exception of about thirty, who would be left to guard the buildings, could be at once detailed for military duty. The command was already organized into a corps of four companies, supported by one section of artillery, and possessing the necessary quantity of ammunition, tents, knapsacks, picks, and shovels. General Smith, the Superintendent, in a letter dated May 2d, to General Breckenridge, who had been placed at the head of all the Confederate troops in the Valley, offered their services for any line of duty to which they might be assigned; but the only purpose to which Breckenridge, in his acceptance, seems to have expected at first to devote them was the old one of "assisting in repelling or capturing the destructive raiding parties," who would soon be operating in many parts of that region. The commanding general evidently thought that the cadets were too young and inexperienced to be attached at once to his main force; but the events of the next few days, and the military necessities of his own position, completely altered his opinion.

On May 4th, anticipating a rapid advance by Sigel in spite of Imboden's opposition, he hurried to Staunton at the head of four thousand men; but it was not until six days later that the Federal General arrived in Woodstock many miles away, his progress having slowed down. Nevertheless, Breckenridge now decided to summon the battalion of cadets to join his army at once, as he considered it likely that small Federal detachments would be sent forward to harry the inhabitants of the middle Valley.

The night the order arrived at the Institute, the long roll was sounded; but as that roll had, during recent months, turned out several times to mean nothing beyond the common, the boys made their way in the darkness to the rendezvous, with only a vague hope of hearing that they were to join immediately the army posted at Staunton. But if there was any listlessness among them from previous disappointment, it was completely shaken out of them by the words of the orders which their Adjutant, surrounded by the other officers, read out by the light of a lantern. The announcement that, under the trusted leadership of its Commandant, Lieutenant-Colonel Scott Shipp, the battalion was to leave next morning to reinforce General Breckenridge, was received with a rousing hurrah from youthful throats that startled the silence of the neighboring hills.

The cadets breakfasted by candle-light the following morning, and then each one, bearing a canteen, haversack, and blanket, fell into rank, the bugle sounded, and accompanied by their battery they set out, with a steady and uniform swing, upon the march to Staunton. One part of their exercises in the Institute had been to tramp about that rough mountain region, and they were thoroughly hardened to the kind of tax which was now about to be put upon their powers of endurance. Raising a cheer as they looked back from a height and got their last view of the turrets of their familiar and well-beloved barracks, they turned again to continue their march, with spirits as lively and steps as elastic as before. Along the country road they advanced all the rest of that day, camping out at night; and the following afternoon, they entered the streets of Staunton, as fresh as sanguine minds and youthful limbs could make them. They must have felt like veterans as they listened to their band responding to the plaudits of the young ladies in a school, under the windows of which they were passing, with the strain, associated with so many wars, of "The Girl I Left Behind Me."

That afternoon, when their dress parade was held in the camp where they stacked their arms, the inhabitants of the town came out apparently en masse to watch the review and to admire the boys in their trim uniforms; and at the dance to which they were invited the same night, they threw the older officers in the shade by their popularity with the ladies. No one would have thought from the gayety of their bearing on that occasion that they had halted in town only for a few hours before taking up the march for the first battlefield of their lives. To every one of them, indeed, it was to prove another ball before Waterloo.

In the midst of all this civilian applause, was it likely that they would grow indignant because the veteran troops broke out, as they swung by in their natty gray coats and bright buttons, with the song "Rock a Bye Baby"?

Couriers having brought in the news that Sigel had left Woodstock and was advancing up the Shenandoah, Breckenridge, as brave a soldier as ever unsheathed a sword, determined, in spite of the disparity between their respective forces, to go forward and attack him as soon as he could come up with him. As his army marched along the road that ran towards Newmarket, where Sigel had arrived, it was strung out in a formidable procession, headed by Echols's brigade, which was followed in turn by Wharton's, the battalion of cadets, the artillery, and the wagon train. The battalion had not yet gone through their baptism of fire, which alone would have entitled them to the post of honor and danger in front.

The army, by the second night, had passed through Harrisonburg and crossed the borders of Shenandoah county. There was now one very conspicuous sign to indicate that they had arrived in a country which had been alarmed by incursions of the enemy – people were met all along the turnpike flying with their families, household goods, horses and cattle to a place of safety. Confederate cavalrymen, belonging to Imboden's small detachment, came up with prisoners who had been captured in brushes with Sigel's vanguard. That night when the troops halted, the cadets could see at a distance the bivouac fires which had been lighted by the pickets and skirmishers who formed the advanced posts of either side. They did not raise any tents to protect themselves from the rain that was now falling, but, with the cheerfulness which distinguished them on their ordinary marches, threw themselves down on the ground to sleep in their blankets until the order to rise should be called out in the morning.

Imboden had been enjoined by General Breckenridge to fall back before Sigel and to take position on the strong line of hills south of the town of Newmarket, in the hope that he might lure the enemy to attack him there; but all his efforts to bring this about proved in vain. When Breckenridge found that his opponents continued immovable, he decided to push boldly up and rush the Federal position in spite of its formidable character; and with this advance in view, he sent an order to his main army to hasten forward to join him. The courier who brought these instructions to the several officers reached Colonel Shipp, in command of the cadets, late at night. At once, they were aroused by word of mouth, as no drum was allowed to be beaten and no call of the bugle to be sounded.

Before the youthful battalion fell in, a prayer was delivered by Captain Preston, who had lost an arm at the Battle of Winchester, and who, though still a young man, had been serving as a subprofessor at the Institute. Here, in the presence of those listening boys, under the broad canopy of the night sky studded with its myriads of sentinel fires, he appealed to the God of Battles in behalf of the youthful soldiers; spoke of the homes and parents they had left behind; of the country whose cause they were about to support so bravely; of the issues of the battlefield, victory or defeat; and of the fate that might overtake each one of them in the great crisis now so close at hand. As soon as this eloquent prayer was finished, the march began in silence, and when the sky indicated the approach of dawn they had passed over the greater part of the ground to be traversed.

As they were swinging along the road in buoyant spirits, they came up with Wharton's brigade of veterans, who at once started to flash their wit at the expense of the boys when the battalion halted near them for a short rest. One of the soldiers, with a pair of shears, moving up and down their ranks, asserted his readiness to cut off love locks to be sent home as souvenirs of those who were about to fall on the field of battle; while another, drawing a mournful face, suggested that orders should now be left for coffins, with the names to be engraved on the plates. The cadets took these ghastly jokes in the humor in which they were uttered, and resumed their march with no damper on their spirits.

Newmarket, their objective, was situated directly on the turnpike from Staunton. West of the town, the land gradually swelled until it looked down in the form of high bluffs on the rushing waters of the North Fork of the Shenandoah. Immediately towards the north, behind the town, the country rose to a height known as Bushong's Hill, while towards the east a terrain of marshes and woodlands culminated in the long and lofty Massanutten mountains. Towards the south, there stood Shirley's Hill, the long northern slope of which gradually sank down almost to the borders of the town. The surrounding country was, for the most part, composed of pastures and wheatfields, divided one from another by fences and stone walls; but between Shirley's Hill and Bushong's Hill, and not far from one side of Newmarket itself, there ran a shallow ravine, which broke the general uniformity of this part of the landscape.

When the battalion reached the vicinity of Newmarket, they deployed behind the screen of Shirley Hill, on the crest of which the Confederate pickets could be seen, and then advanced to occupy the ground assigned them in the arrangements for the impending battle. This was at the extreme left of the line, where they were still concealed from the view of the enemy. While they were taking position, Breckenridge and his staff rode by. The General, a man six feet tall, and strikingly handsome and soldierly in appearance, a superb horseman, and mounted on a noble thoroughbred, seemed to the cheering boys to be the very God of War.

A heavy bombardment was now going on from a Federal battery stationed in a Lutheran church-yard situated just back of the town. The shells passed over the heads of the Federal infantry and fell in front of the advancing Confederates. It was against this battery that the cadets' first participation in the battle occurred.

McLaughlin's artillery, from the meadows near the turnpike, was at the time vigorously replying in support of one of the Confederate brigades which was driving in the Federal skirmishers. The battalion's battery galloped down the turnpike, swerved to the left, and taking a strong position on the slope of Shirley's Hill, in front of the cadets in line, opened in its turn a rapid and effective fire on the Federal guns. The town soon became wrapped in cannon smoke and the intervening space alive with bursting shrapnel.

While all this was happening, the cadets had received orders to cast aside their knapsacks and blankets and to hold their muskets and cartridge boxes in readiness for immediate use. Unconsciously, the boys tightened their belts to ease their movements when the word to advance should ring out. They were not yet directly under fire, but Federal shells, striking the ground on the hill-crest above them, bounded and rebounded by their flank.

In a short time, the Federal battery stationed in the churchyard back of the town, which had been hurling these shells, was compelled to retreat to a higher point in the rear. After a fight in the streets and in the immediate environs of Newmarket, all the Federal forces, which had, in the meanwhile, been reinforced, were drawn back by General Sigel to a second line that rested in part on the brow of Bushong Hill.

Between one and two o'clock in the afternoon, the Confederates received the order to attack. The cadet battalion, which had up to this time been held in reserve – their artillery section alone having so far had any part in the fight – were now commanded to take position in the immediate rear of the advancing brigades of veterans, which soon brought them under fire. Their first intimation of the movement required of them came in the ringing words from Colonel Shipp: "Attention, Battalion, Forward." The sergeant-major, as if the corps was engaged in a dress parade, rushed forty paces in front of it, and had to be made to return to his place on the left of the line. The tall color-bearer shook out the broad folds of his flag to the breeze, and the whole battalion ascended to the crest of the hill with as much calmness and precision as if they were marching forward on the parade ground at Lexington.

So soon as they passed the hill-top, they came in full range of the Federal guns north of the town. Not pausing a moment, they followed the example of the veteran brigade on their right front and moved down the slope at double time. They were now going at a long trot, and before they had covered many yards, a shell burst just ahead of their line, striking with its fragments four of the cadets, who fell to the ground severely wounded. All this while, the brigades of veterans forward and the cadets in the rear were supported by McLaughlin's battery of fourteen pieces advancing on their right along the turnpike and stopping here and there to bombard the town and the Federal positions in its rear.

The new Federal line extended across Bushong's Hill, towards the right, as far as the bluff on the Shenandoah river; while towards the left, it reached as far as the turnpike, on which side it was protected by cedar thickets and woods that spread to the base of the Massanutten mountains. Four hundred yards in front of this strongly posted array of men, General Sigel had stationed two regiments, one of which – that on the left – rested on the turnpike; the other – that on the right – both being in line, joined hands with Von Kleiser's Battery. There was thus a formidable advance force to overcome before the Federal positions behind could be assaulted.

The first success of the Confederates was won by Imboden's troopers, who, with four pieces, pushed close up to the flank of the Federal left wing and compelled the Federal cavalry in that part of the field to retreat. The guns then opened up a very effective fire on Von Kleiser's battery in spite of the long intervening distance. Soon the Confederate brigades, moving towards the enemy's centre, struck this battery and also the two regiments which had been thrown out along with it in front of the main line, and quickly forced both the infantry and the guns to draw back in confusion. In a short while, the Confederates had crossed the abandoned positions and were approaching the slope of Bushong's Hill, the key to the main line itself.

While the Confederate van, composed of the veteran soldiers, were driving the Federal forward line back, the cadet battalion in the rear had left the northern side of Shirley's Hill behind and had passed under the cover of the ravine which lay between the town and the Shenandoah river. Here they halted in order to get ready to take part in the assault which was soon to begin on the enemy's central position in the second line. They threw off all unnecessary equipment and filled their canteens with fresh water from the stream that poured through the hollow.

When the final advance of the whole Confederate army began, the troops on the left and in the right centre, meeting, after they had gone a considerable distance, with a firm resistance from the Federal sharpshooters and batteries, were compelled to stop and to take temporary shelter behind whatever cover the ground afforded. It was a very critical moment. The Confederate army had been checked, and in some places was even falling back, while the enemy were not perceptibly shaken, and were perhaps getting ready to complete the Confederate discomfiture by a charge against their ranks. It was at this juncture, when the issue of the fight was wavering in the balance and the chances for their side were apparently diminishing, that the cadet battalion advanced for the first time to the very front of the battle. They took position in a gap which lay between two of the regiments of veterans. As they came up, they maintained their line with all the exactness of a dress parade. It was noticed by those who were looking on at this splendid spectacle that, in crossing a muddy field, which was of a character to create some confusion among them, the wings swung forward more rapidly than the centre, causing a slight curve in the line at first. Although the cadets were now marching under a heavy artillery fire from the Federal batteries on the heights in front, the officers were able to straighten the line with as little difficulty as if the advance had been in an ordinary field drill; and the battalion proceeded in the same exact order as before.

It was half a mile from the ravine to the Bushong House, the first objective for which they were making. This house stood just at the northern edge of the muddy field through which they were now passing. Behind it was an orchard, and back of this orchard was a wheatfield which fronted the Federal main position. The whole formed the slope and top of Bushong's Hill. When the cadet battalion reached the house, they divided with the same quiet precision as if they were about to move around some obstacle on their parade ground, and came together again behind it without the slightest confusion.

The strongest of all the Federal positions on the second line to which Sigel had retreated was, as we have seen, the one that directly faced these youthful and untried soldiers so soon as they passed around Bushong House. If that portion could be forced, the key to success had been gained. The Federal commander had brought up Von Kleiser's battery, driven back from the first line, and posted it on the hill. Hardly had the cadets come in sight from behind the house when they were exposed to the concentrated fire of several batteries which had an unobstructed view of them from above. The attention of Von Kleiser's guns was temporarily diverted by the assault of a company of Missourians, but before the battalion could reach the northern boundary of the orchard, this battery also was hurling its shells into their midst.

Should they leave the orchard and enter the wheatfield that spread straight up to the position occupied by Von Kleiser? It began to look as if few of the cadets would escape death or wounds. Already the trees in the orchard were being smashed to fragments by the cannon balls. Colonel Shipp was struck and fell severely stunned and bleeding to the ground. A moment of confusion followed. An order passed along the ranks to lie down; all did so, except the ensign, who stood upright waving his flag; and the battalion then began firing under the protection of a worm fence which ran along the northern boundary of the orchard. But the return fire of the enemy was so heavy and accurate that the cry went up, "Fall back and rally on Edgar's battalion." It was a critical moment. Some of the cadets were about to rise to obey, when a first sergeant, Pizzini by name, a Corsican by blood, cocked his rifle and shouted out that he would shoot down the first man who did so. Captain Preston, smilingly resting on his single arm, said that that arm at least he must save. Another Captain, Colonna, spoke encouragingly to the members of his company and directed them to aim coolly and accurately at the enemy.

The first effect of the battalion holding their position was that it relieved the veteran troops on their left from the converging fire of the Federal batteries, and thus gave them the time to reform before renewing the fight with the hostile forces which those batteries were supporting. But before they were ready to advance, General Sigel made an effort to launch a counter-attack. Only one regiment, however, pressed forward to a considerable distance; this was the 34th Massachusetts, which charged almost up to the fence of the orchard where the cadets had halted. Had the latter previously retired from this position, there would have been a gap in the Confederate line at this vital point; the Federal troops would have rushed through; and the whole Confederate army would have been compelled to fall back in disorder.

The tide of battle, which had been running against the Confederates, now suddenly turned. The veterans on the right of the cadets were strongly reinforced; the whole line was firmly reestablished; and an advance was sounded. Colonel Shipp having been disabled, as already mentioned, the battalion was now under the command of their captains. As the order to advance rang out, they leaped up to perform their part in the forward movement. The Federal right had, by this time, been flanked, and the batteries stationed on that part of the Federal line were in retreat. The Federal left had also been driven back. The whole Federal front from one end to the other was soon more or less shaken, but this did not diminish the fire of the Federal battery that looked directly down on the cadets as they passed across the orchard fence and entered the field that led up to the top of Bushong's Hill, on which that battery was posted.

Not long before this final advance began, a black cloud, pregnant with rain, which had been hanging over the field, burst in a terrific downpour. The sheet formed by this deluge, together with the smoke from the Federal batteries, made the air so murky that it was difficult for the eye to distinguish objects some distance ahead. The shells from the battery at the top of the hill had not only to be accurately directed through this half darkness, but had also to stand a further chance of deflection by their downward plunge; but in spite of these hampering influences, their course was sufficiently precise to make the charge of the cadets up to the muzzles of the guns full of flaming peril to all who were participating in it. As they advanced, the Federal battery continued to play upon their line. But the battalion did not halt.

The Federal gunners now began to ram in the shot without using their sponges at all, and the six pieces of artillery in use were worked to their utmost capacity. Still there was no sign of disruption in the line below; here and there, a youthful soldier dropped in his tracks; but the gap was quickly closed up and his comrades came on as firmly and steadily as before. The advance, which had started with a quiet step, had soon increased to a double time, and this at the close had been accelerated to a run.

The Federal gunners, perceiving that they were about to be surrounded and captured, stopped their fire at the last moment and succeeded in getting away with four of the pieces; the remaining two were promptly seized by the battalion. The color sergeant, Evans, leaped upon the caisson of one of these and wildly waved his flag in triumph.

While the cadets were taking possession of the guns, Federal troops, stationed on their right flank in a gully, opened a sharp fusillade on them. The cadets quickly reformed, and wheeling to the right, in their turn opened an equally sharp fusillade on the enemy, and advancing, drove them from the cover of the thickets lying between the spot where the battery had been posted and the turnpike on the eastern side of the battle field. When they finally halted, the whole body of the Federal army had retreated towards the north, followed by the Confederate infantry and cavalry. The last shot of the cadet battalion, like their first, was delivered by their artillery, which now galloped to the top of the nearest hill and hurled numerous shells in the rear of the retiring foe. The fight was finished, and the movement of the Federal forces in the Valley, which had given General Lee at Petersburg serious uneasiness for the time being, was completely frustrated.

That night, the cadets bivouacked in the immediate neighborhood of the veteran brigades, by whom they were now treated with all the respect to which soldiers who had seen real service were entitled. Indeed, all now fraternized on equal terms.

Among the prisoners who were brought into camp was a German soldier, who spoke only imperfect English.

"Dem leetle tevils mit der vite vlag," said he ruefully as he pointed to the cadets, "vas doo mutch for us. Dey shoost smash mine head ven I vas cry zurrender all de dime."

The flag of the battalion, borne aloft throughout the battle, was the one which they always used in their parades at Lexington, and was distinguished by a white and gold ground, with a picture of Washington worked into the centre.

It was asserted at the time that General Breckenridge's Chief of Staff had said to the cadets at the end of the fight, "Young gentlemen, the Commander has you to thank for the day's operations."

But whether this report was correct or not, it is certain that General Breckenridge himself, on numerous after occasions, expressed the conviction that the battalion "had exercised a decisive influence in winning the victory." And this opinion seems to have been justified by at least three events that occurred on that memorable day. First, the battalion had come forward at a critical stage in the course of the fight and filled up a very alarming gap in the Confederate line just where it faced the strongest position occupied by the Federal troops. And secondly, they had held their ground with conspicuous firmness exactly at the moment when confusion was beginning to arise among the Confederate forces stationed on their right, and this tenacity gave those forces an interval in which to restore order and reform. And, lastly, they had repelled the counter charge of a Federal regiment, which, but for their presence at that point, and their ability to resist its onset, would very probably have broken through the Confederate line and compelled that line to fall back in a disastrous retreat.

Five members of the battalion were killed outright; four additional died afterwards of their wounds; while forty-eight received wounds from which they recovered. At least one-fifth of the entire command were disabled.

A very distinguished survivor of the battalion has recorded that, when the men to whom had been assigned the duty of taking up the bodies of the soldiers who fell in the battle, went over the field where these boys – for their average age did not exceed seventeen and a half years – had been brought under the most galling fire, "they found one wearing the chevrons of a first sergeant lying on his face, stiff and stark, with outstretched arms. The next one lay as if asleep; a little fellow, who had torn open his jacket and shirt, and even in death, lay clutching them back, exposing a fair white breast, with its red wound." And not far from him was the body of a third, who, the night before, had confided to a comrade his feeling of certainty that he was destined to meet a soldier's death. One after another they were tenderly lifted and placed on a limber chest and thus carried back to the town, where they were buried with all those military honors which the young heroes had won by the intrepidity of their conduct and the sacrifice of their lives. When the war had come to an end, their remains were exhumed and reverently conveyed to Lexington, and there reburied in the cadets' cemetery, overshadowed by noble oaks, and situated in sight of the Institute where they had received their military training. And a second time, their bodies were removed to a new resting place. They were now buried in the parade ground under the beautiful statue, "Virginia Mourning Her Dead," the work of one who, as a cadet, had been their comrade in the fight. On the anniversary of the Battle of Newmarket, this statue is decorated as a tribute to their memories, and when the roll is called on that day, their names are always included, and as each name is uttered, a cadet steps forward from the ranks and responds, "Dead on the Field of Honor, Sir."

CHAPTER FOURTEEN
The Dash on Baltimore

☆ ☆ ☆ ☆

Among the most hazardous and impetuous adventures that occurred during the war was the raid which Major Harry Gilmor, in July, 1864, at the head of a small company, led to the very environs of the city of Baltimore, which lay at this time far within the enemy's territory and on their principal line of supply between the North and Washington. The railroad which passed through Baltimore from Philadelphia had probably transported more troops to the Federal armies in Virginia than any railway in the United States, and it was guarded by the Federal authorities with sleepless vigilance. To cut this highway even for a short distance would seriously embarrass the Federal plans for reinforcing General Grant, and also might weaken the defenses of the capital. Both of these consummations were, from the Confederate point of view, very desirable at this time, when General Lee was with difficulty holding back the Federal forces in front of Petersburg, and General Early had crossed the Potomac and was moving towards Washington.

Major Gilmor, who undertook to strike this blow at the Federal communications far in the rear of actual fighting, enjoyed a reputation for daring hardly second to that of Colonel Mosby himself; and this new enterprise was not surpassed in its chances of personal peril by any of the ones in which he had previously been

constantly engaged. He possessed but a single advantage in carrying it out, and this might, at any time, become a great disadvan-
tage – the region through which he intended to advance had been
well known to him down to its minutest features from boyhood,
for it was the region where he had been born and reared; but this
very fact, although it might increase his safety during the raid by
furnishing him with assistance of local friends, might also increase
his danger by the probability of his instant recognition by persons
who were hostile to his cause, and ready to inform the authorities
of his presence before report had disclosed it.

But the prospect of being aided by friends and harmed by
enemies among his acquaintances in the dash which he was now
about to make did not influence Major Gilmor in the smallest degree. His design was to tear up the track and burn important
bridges on the Philadelphia and Baltimore Railway; and that purpose he set out, with all the energy and intrepidity for which he
was famous, to carry into effect.

Although, during the first part of the raid, he was followed
at a considerable distance by General Bradley Johnson's brigade,
to which he belonged, yet this brigade furnished no support until
on the point of leaving him. He and his squad of twenty men rode
many miles ahead of this body, and even during the short time it
was following them, they were pursuing an independent enterprise.

When the squad started, they left the brigade at a sharp
gallop, which brought them by sunset to the town of Westminster.
They had learned sometime before arriving there that it was occupied by a large force of the enemy, but instead of this fact causing
them to make a detour, it seemed to arouse a reckless spirit in
their breasts, for, closing up their ranks and drawing their sabres,
they charged pell mell down the main street while they made the
sky ring with their yells. The Federal soldiers posted in the town,
aware that these horsemen were merely the precursors of the large
body of infantry who were following, fired a few shots at the wild
troopers as they came on and then retired in haste to cover. So
great was the speed of the hostile squad that none of the shots hit

their flying mark. There were many citizens of Westminster who sympathized ardently with the Southern cause, and as the Confederate raiders swept past, with shouts and hurrahs. handkerchiefs were waved from numerous windows and responsive cheers were heard above the clatter of hoofs, the yells of defiance, and the explosion of numerous guns and pistols.

That night, Gilmor decided to remain in the neighborhood of the town, as the main body of the Federal forces, apprehensive less they might soon be cut off by Johnson's brigade, had retreated with precipitation along the first road that led to Washington. He, however, took the precaution to sever all the telegraph wires by which Federal reinforcements might be summoned; and he also threw out pickets to prevent a surprise.

The next morning, at an early hour, he started again at the head of his refreshed company. His first objective now was the line of the Northern Central Railway, which formed the principal highway for the transportation of Federal troops and supplies from Harrisburg. This he intended to disrupt by destroying the track for some distance and by setting the torch to the bridges. He had now entered a region of country with which he was familiar and where he knew many persons of importance; but as he rode ahead of his men, mounted on a spirited black charger, he was taken by most of the citizens to be a Federal officer, as it was not conceivable that any Confederate force could have penetrated so far behind the Federal lines. Crossing the Northern Central Railway at Cockeysville, he set fire to the bridge which spanned the Gunpowder river nearby. Baltimore was situated only fifteen miles away.

The brigade, which had been following in his track at a distance, came up with him here, but almost immediately turned back, with the intention of rejoining General Early. General Bradley Johnson, its commander, considered it unwise to risk his artillery by moving farther towards Baltimore. In parting with Gilmor, he assigned him a small additional force to continue the raid.

The region which Gilmor now entered was the immediate scene of his early life, and there was not one hill, valley, or stream that was not associated with his memories of those years; indeed, he could have picked his way through it almost blindfolded. With the aid of his reinforced squadron, he set out from Cockeysville to carry out the main purpose which he had had in view from the beginning, namely, to break up the section of the Baltimore and Philadelphia Railway which lay not far east of the former city. He could now look for no support from any detachment following him; and he was aware that, not only was the railway strongly defended, but the guard could be quickly increased by several regiments dispatched from neighboring posts. This, however, did not cause him for one moment to hesitate to advance towards his desired objective. At first, he took the road that ran straight to Baltimore, but swerving from this highway towards the Gunpowder river again, he stopped at Glen Ellen, the home of his boyhood, where his father and mother still resided

"I captured the whole party on the front steps," he afterwards said laughingly, "and if I except some perhaps just complaints of my rather severe hugging, I treated them with kindness, and upon detainment of a few hours, paroled and released them and moved on with my command."

Such were some of the vicissitudes of the Civil War. The son had nominally at least captured his own parents!

"What is your destination, Harry?" asked a younger member of the family circle, with undisguised concern.

When he had told her, she threw up her hands and exclaimed in a tone of despair, "You will never return alive!"

Major Gilmor for a moment gazed thoughtfully at his small force resting with their horses under the trees.

"I believe you are right," he said quietly. "But I am resolved to fight and to whip everything that stops me."

That night, the small company under his leadership started again on their raid. So exhausted had the men become by the life in the saddle during so many days, with such short interval for repose, that they went to sleep on their horses as they rode along; and Gilmor himself, their guide as well as their commander, was also so overcome by fatigue that he could not resist following their

For this refuge he made with all speed.

example. Suddenly, he was awakened by finding himself surrounded by yelping dogs. The troopers dismounted at the farm house which they had now reached, and they were still so drowsy that they threw themselves at length on the ground and fell at once into a deep slumber.

The next morning, the entire force arose refreshed, breakfasted, mounted, and directed their horses' heads straight for the line of the Philadelphia and Baltimore Railway. As they advanced, Gilmor detailed several soldiers to destroy the telegraph wires that ran beside the highway which they were pursuing. Two others were ordered to ride ahead of the column to look out for Federal pickets. As the two were passing a farmer's house they noticed that a Federal flag was flying over the roof. One of the troopers commanded him to lower it; he declined; and when the trooper attempted to haul it down himself, the farmer discharged a load of buck- shot into his face and breast, and then dropping his gun, fled into the adjacent woods. When the column came up, the trooper, though dying, retained his consciousness and power of speech sufficiently to urge his comrades to leave him behind and to continue at once on their way. Having lifted him into one of his slayer's carts, and given him a cup of water and received his last messages, Gilmor ordered the negro in charge to take the wounded man to the nearest village where a doctor's services were to be obtained.

On the column arriving at the Baltimore and Philadelphia railway, they did not halt to tear up the track first, but pushed rapidly along it towards the bridge that spanned the Gunpowder river; but before they could reach it, they caught the sound of a train approaching from the direction of Baltimore. Gilmor at once ordered a squad of twenty men to go back, and taking a position on either side of the roadbed, to bring the train to a stop by leveling their guns at the engineer. Apprehensive of being shot, and doubtless fearing too that the bridge had been tampered with, this man, as soon as he saw the soldiers, blew his whistle for down-brakes, and the long line of coaches slowed up until they came to a standstill. Guards were at once placed in each car.

"I will shoot or cut down the first man who is guilty of looting," was Gilmor's stern proclamation to the members of his column, and they obeyed him without a question.

It was his intention to compel the engineer to pilot the train as far as Havre de Grace. Having burnt the great railway bridge stretched across the Susquehanna river, he would then return upon his tracks to the Gunpowder river, setting fire to all the bridges in the interval and closing with the destruction of the one spanning the Gunpowder; but before the engineer could be arrested and made to carry out this bold plan, he had leaped from his engine and fled into the woods shutting in the railway at this point.

Informed that General Franklin was aboard of the train, Gilmor in person passed from one end of it to the other in his search for this distinguished officer.

"Is General Franklin in this car?" he inquired in loud tones as he entered each coach.

But there was no reply, although there were many officers to be seen in the different seats.

Starting back from the last car to the first, Gilmor, fully determined to find his man, called out, "Every officer must show his papers."

General Franklin was thus forced to disclose his presence, and he and the other officers were at once removed to the telegraph station nearby and put under a strong guard. While this was being done, the train, all its passengers having left it, was set on fire and completely destroyed. Before the last car had gone up in flames, a second train was heard thundering along from the direction of Baltimore.

This too was stopped, but not before the engineer had leaped from his cab and taken refuge, like the first one, in the under-brush of the adjacent forest, where he could not be followed. As before, no rifling of the passengers' persons and trunks was permitted.

The bridge over the Gunpowder river was defended by a small body of Federal infantry, whom it was necessary for Gilmor to dislodge before burning the structure. On the approach of the Confederate sharp-shooters, they fled to a gunboat which was anchored in the stream. Advantage was at once taken of their retreat – the second train was set on fire, the throttle of the engine opened, and the whole line of cars left to run down to the bridge. The draw was soon filled with coaches that had dropped into the water, and the timbers of the structure broke out in flames. A flag of truce was now sent to the Federal soldiers who had retired to the gunboat, with the request that they would transport to Havre de Grace all the persons who wished to resume their journey northward; and this request was complied with.

The second train having been entirely consumed, the prisoners who were to be carried off were brought forward under a strong guard, and followed by them and by his troopers, Gilmor set out, in high spirits, for Baltimore. His plan was to strike the city on the east, and then to move around its border until he arrived at the entrance to Charles street. Down this street he intended to pass until he should come to its intersection with Franklin; and there turning to the right, it was his purpose to leave the city again by the Franklin turnpike. The route which he would pursue in this programme would lie through the most conspicuous quarter; and this would increase the triumph of the march.

Baltimore, although it had remained in the power of the enemy throughout the war, was still as a whole in sympathy with the Southern cause; and had Gilmor appeared on its most fashionable thoroughfare at the head of his gallant horsemen, he would have been received with such vociferous acclamations as had never before welcomed the presence of a Confederate officer north of the Potomac. But as he approached the city, he was informed that a large body of troops had been hurried thither for its protection, and that, as a further precaution, all the principal streets had been stoutly barricaded. Aware that his force was too small to admit of a chance of success against such serious obstacles, he swerved off when in sight of town and turned his face towards Towson, situated some seven miles away towards the north. Nor did he hesitate in this course when he heard that a squadron of cavalrymen were posted directly in the path which he was following. It was his intention to rush this body as soon as he came up with it, and if unsuccessful, to fall back upon Baltimore, and, under cover of night, to retire through the woods.

As he drew near Towson, he picked out a squad of ten men, and at their head, with pistol in hand, galloped forward to make a reconnoissance. Entering the town at the same speed, but observing no sign of the enemy's presence, Gilmor and his troopers dismounted in front of the tavern and there awaited the arrival of the rest of the column. During this interval, an acquaintance informed him that one thousand horsemen had left Baltimore and were moving forward along the Towson road to intercept his force. He determined to attack the vanguard of this squadron before they could obtain support from their commander coming up behind.

All his men having now assembled in the town square, Gilmor drew them up in a single strong column; and while they were standing quietly in that formation, he sent out a scout to report the first appearance of the hostile cavalrymen. This soldier soon returned with the information that their van was already in sight. A second scout was dispatched, with orders to approach near enough to this advance body to fire on it, and then to return at a gallop to Towson. During his absence, the prisoners were sent off under a guard of ten men, who were instructed, should Gilmor fail to join them after a certain time, to make straight for General Early's army, which was now supposed to be operating in the vicinity of the northern environs of Washington.

As soon as the second scout, having carried out his orders, came back, a squad of fifteen horsemen was sent forward towards Baltimore with instructions to attack the approaching squadron, and after firing their guns, to retreat in a body. Just before they rode up to their comrades posted not far from Towson, they were to divide sufficiently to leave room for a rush by Gilmor and the remainder of his troopers against the Federal detachment, which was certain to be in hurried and confused pursuit.

Although the Confederate raiders were exhausted by their

hard ride and by lack of sleep, and although too they were aware that, in case of defeat even by the Federal vanguard, they could look for no support from behind, still not a voice among them was raised for an immediate and a rapid retreat. The shades of evening were now fast deepening.

"I expect the band will go up tonight," one of the men was overheard to remark, "but we must stick by the Major."

"He will take us through all right," said another. "Only stay by him, and there's no danger."

The troopers pulled their hats closely down on the tops of their heads, and then carefully examined their pistols, which they now held in their hands ready for use. All sat quietly and expectantly in their saddles. Far down the road, they could see their fifteen comrades boldly advancing right up to the heads of the enemy's first row of horses. The sound of firing was heard – the squad had emptied their revolvers in the very faces of the opposing cavalrymen who had replied with a fusillade from their carbines. The Federal vanguard turned back almost at once in great disorder, followed by the yelling Confederate troopers shooting away freely as they pursued; but fearing that they would soon run into the main column, they halted, and then retreated to await the arrival of the rest of the Confederate force, who could be heard approaching at a rapid trot. The darkness was now so great that the latter were unable to distinguish their comrades, and thinking that they really belonged to the enemy, fired on them; fortunately without effect, as the bullets went wild from the inability of the men to take an accurate aim.

The entire Confederate column was now once more united, and Gilmor, having arranged it in proper formation, ordered the whole body to follow him at a gallop as he charged down the road towards the point where the enemy were supposed to have stopped. Shouting at the top of their voices, and making a furious clatter with the hoofs of their horses, they swept forward in the stillness of the night. The Federal cavalrymen, not unnaturally exaggerating their number, very discreetly turned about and retreated in haste towards Baltimore, followed by the Confederate horsemen, firing volley after volley with their pistols into the ranks of the rear guard, who could only be distinguished in the darkness by the flashes of their responding guns. When the pursuers had come within four miles of Baltimore, they halted, and then slowly made their way back to Towson. Not a soldier among them had been killed or wounded, and only one horse had been injured.

No time was now lost by Gilmor in retiring from such a dangerous neighborhood. He set out at once to rejoin General Johnson's brigade, but he had a long distance to traverse before he could hope to come up with it. As his column moved along, the men were overcome with sleep, and some even tumbled from their horses in their slumber. To prevent any loss to his command, Gilmor took a position in the rear, with the intention of picking up those who should fall by the way. But he had not gone far when he lost consciousness himself. How many miles he rode in this condition, he was unable to calculate afterwards. The first sound that awakened him was the jar of a loud voice calling out in the darkness, "Halt, who are you?"

"A friend," replied Gilmor, instantly on the alert.

"A friend to whom?" was the next question expressed in the same threatening tone.

"To the Union," was the firm response.

"What are you doing here at this hour of the night?"

"I have been on a scout after Gilmor's raiders. My captain sent me ahead to tell you that you must not fire on his men."

"Very well, I won't do so."

"I will return at once and inform him that the road is safe," said Gilmor, wheeling his horse's head to the right about.

He soon perceived that, while asleep, he had passed out of the main road into a country byway. Leaping a fence and making across the fields, he was soon once more in the right track, along which he now advanced at a gallop in order to catch up with the members of his command. Discovering one of his men asleep by the roadside, he halted and dismounted to awake him. The soldier, on being shaken into full consciousness, informed him that he had been left there to tell him that the rest of the column was resting at a spot a short distance off. When the two reached this spot, all the men were seen lying on the ground buried in slumber; at once, they were aroused; and the entire body set out for the place which had been assigned as the rendezvous when the guard in charge of the prisoners departed from Towson. On arriving there, they found the guard and prisoners fast asleep, but the buggy in which General Franklin had been driving was empty.

"Where is General Franklin?" exclaimed Gilmor in tones of anger. "I ordered him to be kept under a constant guard in the buggy."

"He is in the fence corner sleeping with the other prisoners," was the reply.

But an investigation there did not disclose the presence of the distinguished Federal officer; he had really taken advantage of the drowsiness of his captors to escape into the wood; and it was to no purpose that scouts were sent out in every direction to bring him back – not a trace of him was to be detected. Gilmor, hoping that he might discover papers of value in the General's valise, ordered it to be opened and its contents examined, but they were found to consist only of a prayer book, a snuff box, and several photographs; all of which were, at a later date, returned to the owner.

As soon as the column set out again, Gilmor, whose slumbers had been interrupted, went to sleep on horseback. One of his troopers rode at his side to prevent his falling to the ground as he passed along. Two Confederate sympathizers interviewed him while he was in this condition of irrepressible drowsiness; he talked with them in a disjected manner, but afterwards had no recollection of a single question asked or what had been his reply. At the end of this profound slumber, he awoke refreshed, and on the second day galloped, at the head of his men, into the camp where his brigade, under General Bradley Johnson, had temporarily halted.

CHAPTER FIFTEEN
Lieutenant Wise Carries the Message to Lee

☆　☆　☆　☆

Clover was a little village situated about a hundred miles southwest of Richmond, on the railroad running to Danville. This railroad was now of the last importance to the Confederacy, not only because it was the principal artery of supply for the troops defending the lines at Petersburg, but also because, should those troops be compelled to evacuate these lines, it would become the highway by which they, in their retreat, would endeavor to join the army in North Carolina under General Johnston. The village had some military value as being only a few miles distant from the bridge over the Staunton river, which had to be kept under a strong guard so as to assure the safe passage of trains to Petersburg and Richmond from the granaries and conscript depots of the South. It was the gateway also to a region of country which still furnished a large quantity of food for the Confederate army, mules for its wagon trains, and slaves to work on the fortifications at the front.

On Sunday morning, April 2d, 1865, a small band of Confederate officers had gathered in the Clover railway station to obtain any news that might be passing over the wires. This had become a habit with them for some time, as events of supreme importance were now taking place at Petersburg which might at any moment fatally compromise the entire position of the Confederacy; but it was with a keener anxiety than usual that they entered the office that morning, for, on the previous day, a dispatch had been received which stated that General Sheridan had routed the Confederate right-wing at Five Forks, and was about to cut the Confederate army off from their shortest road to the South, should they be compelled, as now seemed certain, to abandon their trenches.

It was not until eleven o'clock in the day that messages began to pour over the wires, and as each was caught by the operator and repeated to the persons standing around him, it seemed to be of a blacker significance than the one that went before. The first to come in was: the lines at Petersburg were broken this morning; the second: General Lee is retiring from the city; the third: the Confederate army is retreating towards Amelia Court-House on the Richmond and Danville Railroad; and finally: orders have been issued for the immediate evacuation of Richmond.

Two events were now confidently expected by the officers, who, in spite of the gloomy news which they had just received, declined to despond, namely, that Mr. Davis and his cabinet would be passing southward through Clover within twenty-four hours; and that before a week had passed, General Lee and his troops would cross Staunton river by the bridge a few miles away and slowly fall back towards the Carolinas.

The first event took place precisely as anticipated – Mr. Davis, accompanied by his chief civil advisers, appeared on the following morning in a train which had been specially reserved for his party, and after a short stop, continued his journey towards Danville, where, reestablishing the seat of government, he remained for several days. Would Lee too come along to serve with his army as a shield of defense between these heads of the central administration and the pursuing enemy?

All the rest of Monday, all Tuesday, and down to midday, Wednesday, most of the patient watchers kept their seats, until they were worn out by fatigue and the stress of anxiety. Not a message arrived from any point situated beyond Burkeville; not a message from any point this side which gave any information as to the movements of the Confederate army. All trains had ceased to run. The ominous silence was unbroken and impenetrable.

Then suddenly there came a telegram from Burkeville announcing that the wires between that village and Amelia Court-House, where General Lee was known to have arrived in his effort to get astride of the Richmond and Danville railroad, had been cut; and that it was reported that Federal cavalry had possession of the line between the two stations. This rumor, if true, signified that the Confederate army had been compelled by superior power to abandon their original objective, and to strike across the country to Farmville, with the expectation of continuing their retreat by the Southside Railway towards Lynchburg.

General Walker, who was the officer in command at Clover, promptly informed Mr. Davis at Danville of the rupture of the telegraph line beyond Burkeville. Mr. Davis was still hopeful that General Lee had not been forced to swerve from his intended course; but in order to ascertain definitely where he was, and what were his plans for the immediate future, the President requested General Walker to let him know whether he had a trustworthy officer who would volunteer to pass in an engine as far down the railway towards Richmond as it would be necessary to go before coming up with the Confederate troops.

It happened that, when the President's message was received by General Walker, Lieutenant John S. Wise alone was present with him, and he at once volunteered to go in search of General Lee and to obtain from him the information desired. The Lieutenant had been one of the cadets who had taken part in the Battle of New Market, where he had been wounded, and he was still a mere boy in years as well as a stripling in appearance.

"You are too young," said General Walker decisively when the young officer offered his services.

In a short time, however, he reconsidered his refusal. But it was probably the impression which he had of the youthfulness of the messenger, and of the rashness usual with that period of life, that led the veteran officer to dwell at length on the necessity for excessive caution at every stage of the journey. His instructions to the young man were almost minute in their details. If, on arriving at Burkeville, he should find that the enemy had not yet reached that station, then he was to use his own judgment as to passing with his engine to the track of the Southside Railway – which crossed the Danville Railway there – and moving down that road until he should catch up with the retreating Confederate army. If the Southside Railway too had been seized in part by the enemy, then he must obtain a horse and make his way across the country to General Lee's headquarters.

General Walker himself was convinced that the Federal advance guard had really taken possession of Burkeville.

"My reason for thinking so," he remarked, "is that this evening, after a long silence, we have received several telegrams purporting to be from General Lee urging the forwarding of stores to that point. From the language used, I am satisfied that it is a trick to capture the trains. But I may be mistaken. You must be careful to find out the facts before you get to the place."

About nightfall of the same day, an engine, with a baggage car attached, arrived from Danville with important papers from Mr. Davis; and Lieutenant Wise, accompanied by General Walker, went to the station to get aboard of it. The General, as if still disposed to fear lest so youthful a messenger should act rashly and expose himself to avoidable danger because failing to evince the cautious spirit which an older head would be careful to show, again urged upon him the need of the utmost prudence and discretion in every step which he should take in the dangerous expedition before him. But that he intended that the whole responsibility for every movement should rest upon the young officer was revealed by his parting words to the engineer.

"Remember," he said to him, "you are to obey implicitly every command of Lieutenant Wise."

The Lieutenant had, by this time, thrown a couple of blankets into the car to serve as a rude bed. Having thrust a revolver into his hip pocket and placed numerous cartridges in his haversack, he buttoned up closely in his breast pocket the sign manual empowering him to impress a horse if necessary, and also the autograph order for General Lee, both of which he had just received from Mr. Davis. After a few more words with General Walker, he mounted into the car and gave the engineer the signal to start.

The night sky was overcast with clouds, but every now and then through a rift the moon would shine out, spreading a ghostly light over the broken face of the country, and then would vanish again behind the black veil, leaving the fields and woods adjacent to the railway buried once more in darkness. There was no lamp at the head of the engine to cast a narrow yellow beam far down the rails as the wheels clattered along; and not even a candle was burning in the car occupied by the single passenger. Occasionally, as the furnace door was opened to receive another supply of fuel, the flare of the fires within would, for a minute, illumine the cab and play around the grim and swarthy figures of the engineer and fireman; but soon, with a sharp bang, the entrance to the small inferno in the bowels of the locomotive would be closed, and the men would be swallowed up again in the blackness.

It was a lonely region through which the engine and car were passing. For a century, it had been the chief seat in Virginia of tobacco culture and slave holding, and was divided up into large plantations, which had dispersed the inhabitants and left the far greater proportion of the surface of the soil to grow up in bushes and dwarfed woods. War too had affected it by making the population still more sparse and compelling the abandonment of still wider spaces of the land. As the short train moved on along the track the only sound that broke the deep stillness of the country was the rattle of the engine and car. Not a light was to be seen shining from the windows of a cabin or mansion to show the proximity of human beings; not a single cry was to be heard that indicated the presence of a watch dog or of some hunter abroad with his hounds in the forest. The entire land and all its inhabitants seemed to be wrapped in awed silence, which may well have fallen on them under the influence of the great events that were now crowding upon each other on the theatre of the war for the doom of the Confederate cause.

The stillness and the darkness were brought home all the

more impressively by the slowness with which the engineer was compelled to move owing to the dangerous condition of the track, which, at some places, consisted simply of wooden rails covered over with scrap iron. The stations were situated far apart, and as they were passed, offered not a single sign of human life. Whenever the wood and water sank so low in the tender that it was necessary to renew the supply, Lieutenant Wise, the engineer, and the fireman were forced to do the work without assistance; the negro station-hands had all vanished; and every station-master had apparently followed their example, in their expectation of the enemy's early arrival.

After leaving Clover, the engine and car ran for some distance through a large body of thick woods, and then entering the open country, descended by a sharp grade to the bridge over the Staunton river. At this spot, for the defense of the structure, extensive earthworks had been thrown up; and they had proved fully effective in the battle which had taken place there only a few months before, on which occasion the dangerous raid of General Wilson had been brought to a dead stop. That officer, at the head of a large detachment, had advanced from Petersburg to this point, which was far behind the Confederate lines; but on reaching it, he was signally defeated; and when he endeavored to return, was driven in confusion towards the south.

Having clattered through the closed-in-bridge – the muddy surface of the stream below being barely visible between the sills of the track – the train then passed along the tall embankment that carried the rails across the broad lowgrounds to the edge of the hills. It then entered the gap through which the Little Roanoke poured down from the uplands of the back country to join the Staunton; then it rattled on by the banks of numerous brooks and creeks that offered, in the midst of the rough landscape, a narrow stretch of level ground. Onward still it rolled between long ridges that rose bare or wooded on either side of the way; through the wide open fields, where no object as yet could be distinguished; through deep cuts, where the earth had been torn apart with shovel and pick to produce a uniform grade; and through almost endless lengths of forest that stood black and silent on either hand. Mile upon mile, the wheels rattled on, and slowly the train drew nearer and nearer to Burkeville, the place upon which all the thoughts of Lieutenant Wise and the engineer were concentrated.

It was two o'clock in the morning when they arrived at Meherrin, situated only twelve miles away from their objective. Here the engine and car having been brought to a stop, Lieutenant Wise jumped to the platform to find out whether he could arouse anyone in the houses that loomed in the darkness back of the station. The station itself was entirely vacant. He banged away at the door of the first house which he reached, but no one responded to his blows in spite of their loudness. Again he knocked with redoubled energy.

"Who's thar?" came a muffled voice, as if from beneath bed clothes within.

"A friend," was the reply, given quietly but firmly.

An old man poked his head cautiously out of the window.

"Have you heard anything from Lee's army?"

"Naw, nothin' at all. I heerd he was at Amely Cote House yistiddy."

"Have you heard or seen any Yankees here-abouts?"

"None here yit – I heerd thar was some at Green Bay yistiddy, but they have done gone back."

"Back where?"

"I dunno. Back to Grant's army, I reckon."

"Where is Grant's army?"

"Lord knows. It pears to me like its everywhar. I seed a man come by here late yistiddy, and he said he come from Burkeville, so I reckon thar warn't none thar when he lef, but whether they is come since I can't say."

One fact at least Lieutenant Wise found out from this conversation – General Lee was certainly not at Burkeville. Was any detachment of General Grant's army there? That was a question which only actual investigation could answer correctly. All the chances were, that, if Lee had been thrust away from the Richmond and Danville road, as seemed now highly probably, Burkeville was in the possession of Federal outposts at least; and the presence there of even so small a force as that would make an approach to the place by three Confederates quite as dangerous as though many thousand troops were encamped in the neighborhood.

However, it was essential that he should find out positively whether Burkeville was held by Federal soldiers, for, until this was actually proved, he could not decide upon the proper course for him to follow in carrying out his orders to reach the Confederate army. If they did not hold it, he could switch the engine and car to the Southside Railway and go on to Farmville, which lay in the path of Lee's possible advance. If they did hold it, then he could return to Meherrin, impress a horse, and make straight across the open country.

Mounting to his car again, Lieutenant Wise gave the signal to the engineer to move forward. Four miles further up the railway was another station, and here he ordered the train to be again stopped. This place was more hushed and deserted than Meherrin; not a single person was to be found there; and he drew the conclusion that all had fled under the influence of a report that the Federal vanguard was not far away. As he stood there in the darkness and silence, a whippoorwill began to utter its cry in a neighboring swamp, and the sound, always gruesome and melancholy, seemed to deepen the loneliness of the surrounding country as well as to emphasize the hopelessness of the Confederate cause, pursued even into that remote corner of the land by overwhelming force.

"Go very slowly," was the order which Lieutenant Wise now gave the engineer; and both set themselves to watch more carefully than ever for the first indications of the enemy's presence. Burkeville was situated only eight miles away, but even eight miles is a considerable space when the wheels of an engine are made to revolve at a very low rate of speed. As they drew near to the place, they observed the reflection, as if from a fire, in the sky ahead of them; but as the track followed a curve in approaching the village, and was also shut in on both sides by thickets of pine and small oaks, it was impossible at that distance to discover the origin of the suspicious light. Was it due to the fires in the enemy's camp, or had a detachment of Lee's army after all been able to march this far in their retreat? But why, at this late hour, should either friend or foe keep up camp fires of such a size, or in such number, as to throw a bright reflection like that on the face of the heavens?

What should now be the next step for the Lieutenant to take? Should he creep through the underbrush until he should come in sight of the fires, and thus be able to find out what caused them, or should he remain on the engine and go forward to the very point where the fires were burning? If he stole through the bushes, much time would be lost, although that course would be the safer of the two to follow. On the other hand, if he advanced by rail, he could reach the immediate vicinity of the place within a few minutes, and there would be a fair chance that the engine could be reversed in time, if necessary, and an escape quickly made.

He decided to go forward by rail, but when he announced his decision to the engineer, the latter protested against it with vehemence.

"What, Lieutenant," he exclaimed, "ain't you afraid they are Yankees? If they are, we are goners."

Lieutenant Wise declined to yield. The engineer, still muttering his objections, reluctantly drew back the lever, and the engine and car, which had been stopped, again moved slowly forward along the rails. A sharp turn in the track brought them in full view of the Burkeville station. At once, the cause of the light reflected on the sky was explained – large gangs of workingmen were employed, in the flare of many torches, in tearing up the track of the Southside Railway, which crossed the Richmond and Danville at this point. In reality, they were changing the gauge in order to facilitate the transfer of Federal troops and munitions from Petersburg to aid in cutting off the advancing Confederates before they should arrive at Farmville.

One glance revealed to Lieutenant Wise that he was in the presence of the enemy; and hardly had that thought flashed through

through his mind when his own presence was observed by the Federal guards. The clatter of the wheels had passed unnoticed owing to the noise made by the tools of the workingmen; but as soon as the engine turned the curve, the light from the torches was reflected on its metal front and side, and it stood fully disclosed to view, a conspicuous, and the enemy would be sure to think, a hostile object. There was not a moment to be lost by its occupants if they were to escape with their lives.

"Reverse the engine," called out Lieutenant Wise to the engineer peremptorily.

The man seemed for the moment to be paralyzed by the danger of his situation, and made not the slightest movement to obey the order.

"It's no use," he replied in blubbering tones. "They will kill us before we can get under way."

"Reverse the engine or you are a dead man," the Lieutenant hissed, clapping the muzzle of his pistol to the engineer's ear as he spoke.

The engineer, as if galvanized into activity, once more drew back the lever, and the engine slowly responded.

The Federal guards had approached so near that they could be heard crying out "surrender, surrender." The wheels were now moving more rapidly. "Surrender, surrender," the call was reiterated. Still more rapidly moved the wheels. A volley was fired and the bullets rattled against the sides of the engine, cab, and tender. The fireman had hidden himself in the tender, while Lieutenant Wise and the engineer had thrown themselves down on the floor of the cab. Within a few minutes, the engine had acquired sufficient speed to bear them beyond the danger zone, and after a while had to be slowed down to prevent it jumping the rickety track. But the engineer for one did not seem to be elated by his escape from the enemy; indeed, in spite of his duties at the throttle, he appeared to be ruminating sadly on some subject that possessed his mind. Turning at last to Lieutenant Wise, he said, in the whining voice peculiar to persons of his social class in the South, "Lieutenant, would you have blowed my brains out sho' nuff if I hadn't done what you told me?"

"Certainly I would," replied Lieutenant Wise.

"Wall," said the engineer turning again to his throttle, with a sigh, "all I've got to say is, I don't want to travel with you no mo'."

"You'll not have to travel far. I shall get off at Meherrin and you can go back."

"What," exclaimed the engineer, "you goin' to get off at Meherrin in the dark by yourself, with no hoss and right in the middle of the Yankees? Darn my skin if I'd do it for Jeff Davis hisself."

Dawn had just begun to appear when the engine, with its single car, came to a full stop at Meherrin and Lieutenant Wise descended to the platform. It was his intention to travel across the country until he should reach General Lee's temporary headquarters, wherever they might be. There was no doubt now that the Confederate army was advancing towards Farmville, but how far towards that town had it progressed? Had Federal troops been able to head them off by following the Southside Railway? If the Lieutenant set out to push his way through the countryside to Farmville, would he not be in danger of running into this intervening cordon of Federal soldiers? Indeed, was it possible to ride around them at all, no matter how wide the detour which he might make? Would not the same barrier confront him at every point? But he was under positive orders to bear Mr. Davis's message to General Lee on horseback if the engine could not safely go as far as Burkeville; and however dangerous the journey over land might be, or how uncertain the chance of reaching the Confederate army, he resolved to discharge his duty at all hazards.

Having instructed the engineer to report to General Walker a full account of what had been seen at Burkeville, and also to inform him of the proposed ride across country, Lieutenant Wise gave him, for the last time, the signal to move on, and then turned away to find out whether he could procure a horse to carry him on the perilous mission with which he had been intrusted. Not a horse was to be obtained. Anticipating the early arrival of the

Federal stragglers, the people about the station had taken the pre-caution to send off to a distance all the horses which they owned as the only means of preventing their seizure by the enemy.

But the Lieutenant was not to be discouraged; he set out on foot in the direction of Farmville, with the hope that he might be able, when he had gone further into the country, to discover a riding horse which he might impress. He had walked perhaps several miles along the road leading through the forest when he came to an opening where there were fields under cultivation; and just at the side of the highway as it was about to plunge again into the woods, he saw a farmer's house, and directly in front of this house, tied to a rack, he noticed what appeared to be a young and vigorous horse already saddled and standing there seemingly awaiting his arrival to carry him forward to his destination. But he could not go and deliberately mount the animal and ride away without a word to its owner, who probably resided in the house.

Not having eaten that day, he was, by this time, very hungry after his walk, and under the influence of this additional reason for interviewing the farmer, he boldly knocked at the door, and gladly accepted the invitation to enter which was at once hospitably extended to him. Breakfast had already been put on the table, and besides the farmer – a man above the military age – and his family, he found a Confederate cavalryman, who proved to be the owner of the horse. This soldier, having recently lost one in the service, had returned to his home in the neighboring county to obtain another, and was now on his way to rejoin the Confederate army.

"I require your horse and must have it," said Lieutenant Wise abruptly.

The trooper's only reply was a careless laugh, as he supposed the stranger was amusing the company with a joke.

The Lieutenant coolly took from his pocket the sign manual which Mr. Davis had sent him, through General Walker, and quietly handed it to the soldier.

"You will observe," said he, "that I am empowered to impress a horse, should it become necessary."

He then explained the mission which he had been ordered to discharge, and the cavalryman, with chagrin but without further demur, consented to the appropriation of his horse.

Lieutenant Wise, having finished an excellent breakfast, mounted the animal and started upon his journey again, with refreshed vigor and highly-sanguine spirits, in spite of the fact that the farmer had just told him that Sheridan's troopers had already been seen in the neighborhood. Advancing with eyes and ears wide open to detect any sign of the enemy's proximity, it was not long before he began to hear the reverberation of heavy guns toward the northeast, which might be at no great distance away; this led him to turn into a road that ran in a more westerly direction than the one which he had been following; but he had gone only a few hundred yards along it when he caught the sound of numerous horses' hoofs behind him, and, on looking back, he saw a column of Federal cavalrymen advancing towards him. When they perceived that their presence had been detected, they started in hot pursuit of him, and as they did so, they fired a volley at him, in the hope of bringing him and his horse to the ground; but the animal, being strong and fresh, in a few minutes carried him beyond the range of their shots.

As Lieutenant Wise was congratulating himself that he had escaped by his horse's fleetness, he beheld in front of him, far down the vista of the highway along which he was galloping, another column of Federal troopers, who had just begun to debouch from a by-road. At that distance, they evidently mistook him at first for a comrade, for they neither sent out scouts to intercept him nor raised their guns to shoot at him.

He now found himself in a predicament. If he advanced, he would run directly into the teeth of the column in front; if he retreated, he would, with equal certainty, fall into the jaws of the column behind. In his perplexity, he stopped his horse, and this action at once aroused the enemy's suspicion; several troopers promptly left the main detachment and advanced towards him; and even raised their guns and fired at him. Wheeling his horse's head towards the side of the road and clapping his heels into his flanks. Lieutenant Wise was, in a second, carried into the woods out of sight, and a run of half a mile among the trees brought him beyond the reach of pursuit.

It was now clear to him that it was only by bending farther to the west that he could hope to avoid the numerous columns of the enemy who were working around the wings of the retreating Confederate army. Keeping still to the protection of the forest, he was moving forward in a westerly direction when suddenly a man in Confederate uniform with carbine in hand, appeared from behind a large oak.

"Halt," he cried, leveling his gun at the horseman as he spoke, "who are you?"

Lieutenant Wise's instant impression was that the man before him belonged to the order of Federal soldiers popularly known as Jesse scouts, a class that always wore the Confederate uniform, and, being in reality spies and expecting no mercy when captured, were notoriously ruthless and lawless. Feeling sure that this impression was a correct one, he was at first inclined to dissemble, but, fortunately for himself, he frankly gave his name and stated his rank. It was a Confederate scout who confronted him.

"What the devil are you doing here?" the scout exclaimed as he lowered his carbine.

He too had taken the horseman for a Jesse scout, and was equally relieved to find that he had, not an unscrupulous enemy, but a comrade in misfortune before him. Lieutenant Wise fully explained the mission which he had to carry out.

"I will help you," responded the scout heartily. "The Yankees are all around us. Wait one minute."

He disappeared behind the screen of the underbrush, and when he came out again, he was mounted on a handsome horse, which he had been keeping under cover. He had evidently a perfect knowledge of the woods in front, for he advanced without hesitation.

"I am one of General Rooney Lee's scouts," he said in reply to Lieutenant Wise's inquiry. "I have been hanging on the enemy's flank for several days."

"You gave me a great fright," said Lieutenant Wise, "I thought you were a Yankee sure, and I came near telling you that I was one."

"It was well that you did not," replied the scout, "I am taking no prisoners on this trip."

He tapped the butt of his carbine significantly.

The two men rode on together until they came to the edge of the forest, where they were able to command an extensive view of the country sloping down towards one of the larger affluents of the Appomattox river. In the distance, they could see a Federal column descending to the very ford by which the two Confederates intended to cross; and in order to anticipate the enemy in this action, Lieutenant Wise and the scout pressed their horses forward at a double rate of speed, and did not halt until they reached a thickly wooded hill that overlooked the ford.

"Stop here one moment, while I ride out to see whether we can cross safely," said the scout.

After advancing some distance ahead in the open, he waved his hand to the horseman behind to signal to him to come on and then galloped down to the stream. Lieutenant Wise quickly followed. The column of Federal cavalrymen had soon observed their movements and set out in pursuit. The scout crossed the ford in safety, but before his companion could do so, he became the target for a fusillade of shots, which, fortunately for him, fell short of the object they were aimed at. He had bent far over and nestled close under his horse's shoulder in order to escape the bullets; and he was further protected by the continuous fire which the scout and numerous pickets, posted behind a turn in the road on the further bank of the river, kept up in reply to the Federal volleys.

Leaving the water, with his horse still unwounded, he quickly found shelter behind a hill that rose at the side of the highway. Without further danger, and still accompanied by the scout, he made his way to Farmville; but the hour of midnight passed before he was able to hand his autograph order to General Lee and explain in person the mission upon which he had been sent by

Mr. Davis.

CHAPTER SIXTEEN
How the Colonel Saved the Town

☆　☆　☆　☆

During the four years of war, the town of Danville, Virginia, was somewhat remote from the scenes of actual fighting, and certainly partly from this fact was chosen as the site for one of the most important military prisons in the Confederacy. But there was another reason why it was thought to be suitable for such a prison – it contained many tobacco warehouses of a large size which could be easily converted into convenient buildings for the detention of captives. At all times, there were from six to seven thousand Federal soldiers penned up here; and this small army had rather increased than fallen off in number as the end of hostilities drew near. Even after General Lee had surrendered at Appomattox, the doors still remained closed, and the captives within were for some time longer debarred from freedom.

During the existence of this crowded prison, it was guarded partly by disabled Confederate soldiers, partly by men too old to serve actively in the army, and partly by boys too young. The person at the top responsible for the safe keeping of all these captives, and for the discipline of the squads that stood as sentinels over them, was Colonel Robert E. Withers, a gallant and imposing officer, who had been shot more than once through the body, and who had not been able to recover sufficiently from his last wound to return to his command in the field.

Among the numerous difficulties with which he had constantly to contend was the shortage in the food supply, a condition
which steadily grew more serious even for the citizens of the town
as the war drew slowly to a conclusion. The wealthiest began to
feel the pinch. Meat, even by them, was only eaten once in twenty-
four hours; and quite frequently it was, for a time, not obtainable
at all. Colonel Withers himself, the most influential person in the
community and occupying the highest official position there, was
only able to procure enough from day to day to satisfy the needs
of a delicate daughter under age. This portion was thrown into the
pot along with a large quantity of black-eye peas, so that the peas
might absorb its flavor and thus prove more nourishing to the
elders, who made their dinner on this and other vegetables; followed, as a sweetmeat, by bread and sorghum molasses. There
was at least an abundance of rice, since that staple continued
throughout the war to be cultivated in the South.

Amidst this universal dearth, the prisoners naturally fared
the worse; and there were times when they lacked the necessary
quantity even of the coarse food which was given out to them
from day to day. The negroes were not reduced to such straits, for
they foraged furtively on their own hook; and not a single recepta-
cle of food, whether belonging to their masters or to other people,
was safe from their intrusive fingers and hungry stomachs. On one
occasion. Colonel Withers visited Mrs. Stuart, the mother of the
famous Confederate Cavalry General, who resided in Danville, and
to his surprise, found a very fat turkey tied by the leg to a handsome rosewood bedstead in the principal sleeping chamber.

"Why do you keep this noble bird in your best room?" he
asked, with a laugh.

"It's a Christmas present from friends in the country," was
the reply. "If I turned it out in the yard, it would be stolen before
night."

As the winter of 1864-5, the last and most harrowing of
the war, dragged on to an end, and the military outlook grew
more desperate from shortage of men and food, the situation of
the people of Danville and the prisoners became steadily more dis-

tressing and intolerable. The spring opened with no promise whatever of relief, unless it was to come with the collapse of the Confederacy, which now seemed to be impending. Early in April, the news was received that General Lee had abandoned the trenches around Petersburg, which his troops had been holding so valiantly in spite of hunger and disparity in numbers.

"Richmond has been evacuated," was the next message that flashed over the wires; and on the following morning, Mr. Davis and his cabinet arrived; but this only served to deepen the prevailing gloom, as their withdrawal from the capital indicated the low ebb to which the Confederacy had fallen. A few days later, the report spread that General Lee had surrendered, and the probability of its truth was supported by what was told by soldiers, passing through the town, who had left the army for one reason or another before it reached Appomattox. Any doubt which was felt at first as to the accuracy of the rumor rapidly grew less and less, without, however, diminishing the sense of uncertainty about the future which was now shared by all.

Not long after Mr. Davis and his advisers had left for the South, a Confederate General, at the head of a considerable body of veteran cavalrymen, rode into town and publicly announced that he had been ordered to burn the bridges across the river, and also to destroy the Confederate stores of all sorts that had been collected in the warehouses. Had all this been done, Danville would have suffered precisely the fate which had just overtaken Richmond – an inextinguishable conflagration would have followed, and the whole town would, in the end, have been consumed. As the Confederacy had now given up the ghost in Virginia at least, not the smallest military advantage would have accrued from such universal ruin.

The first man to recognize this fact was Colonel Withers; and instead of standing helplessly by and seeing thousands of people rendered wantonly homeless, and millions of dollars in property given over to the torch for a mere delusion, he came forward boldly to face the military authority and to oppose the consummation of such an act of folly as was intended. Apart from his conviction as to the uselessness of such destruction at this hopeless hour, he had reason to apprehend that, as the fires should spread, the thousands of prisoners, maddened by their hunger and thirsting for retaliation, would have to be released; and when thus turned loose, would overrun the streets in a spirit to commit every outrage which the situation permitted and invited. He forcibly pointed out to the Confederate officer the certainty of these disasters, should he insist on burning the bridges and the stores in the warehouses.

"I have my orders. Colonel," was the reply. "I have no option. I must carry them out."

"Even if you burn the bridges, General," remonstrated Colonel Withers, "a Federal army can pass by the ford a short distance down the stream. Why then destroy these bridges which our people need hourly and cannot replace?"

But the General was immovable. Colonel Withers returned to the prison and at once ordered a company of picked guards to march to the principal bridge and protect it with musketry, should an attempt be made to set it on fire. When a small detachment of regular soldiers approached for the purpose, they were sternly warned by the captain of the squad to halt, and the butts of guns were brought to the shoulder to shoot as soon as the word was given. The officer of the detachment, perceiving that he was about to be resisted to the death, commanded his men to face about and return to headquarters. No further effort was made to destroy the bridges.

But the General, still obedient, like the soldier and not the citizen, to his orders from an authority which had now passed away, next took steps to ply the torch to all the stores housed in Danville. As a large proportion of them consisted of liquors of various kinds, there was no ground for objecting to their destruction – indeed it was advisable that, in that hour of license and confusion, they should be put out of the way – but it was necessary that this should be done in a manner that would not endanger the safety of the town. A warehouse full of wines and the like inflammable articles would be certain to scatter the conflagration at the

The largest store-house in the town was on fire.

very start far and wide, and, in the end, would wrap every building in flames.

Again Colonel Withers protested, and this time success-fully. But that night, after he had gone to bed, he was awakened with the news that the largest store-house in the town was on fire. Leaping from his bed, and hardly stopping to put on all his clothes, he hastened to the General's headquarters, and in lan-guage that was not at all minced reproached him with violating his promise. But in this he was unjust, for the General proved to him that the fire had been caused, not by a match set to the outside of the storehouse, but by an explosion of alcohol within it; the men with candles, who were staving in the barrels, had inadvertently knocked in the head of a cask of alcohol, and the vapor, at once igniting, had thrown the whole interior of the building into flames that could not be put out. The explosion had instantly killed the officer who was superintending the work of destruction. As the night was calm, the fire was prevented from spreading to the sur-rounding houses.

Within a few days, the General and his cavalry-men rode away to North Carolina. But hardly had they vanished, when many of the soldiers who had been paroled at Appomattox began to arrive in town on their way to their homes in the States situated further south. Throughout the winter and early spring, these men had been cooped up in the trenches of Petersburg, where they had endured the most acute hardships from lack of proper food and clothing. When the retreat began, they expected to find a large supply of rations awaiting them at Amelia Court-House; but when they reached that place the only provisions which they had to eat were the scanty quantity that had been obtained by scouring the already famished countryside.

Nor did their situation improve in this respect as they marched towards Appomattox; the intervening region, being sparsely inhabited and poorly cultivated, furnished only the slim-mest rations for the men and the most meagre forage for the horses. In the history of war, few great armies have come as near actual starvation as this one did in the last stage of the retreat; and it was not until the surrender had taken place, and the contents of the supply trains, intercepted by the Federal cavalry, had been distributed among the soldiers, that they at last got enough to satisfy their hunger.

The country between Appomattox and Danville, through which many of the disbanded Confederates were compelled to pass on their way homeward, was never a thickly populated region; it was, in fact, divided for the most part into large estates, which had been thoroughly drained of wheat, corn, and hay by the long trains of canvas-topped wagons that gathered up supplies for the army. It happened that the end of the war came, not only when all the crops of the previous season had been carried off, but also when the crops of the new either had not ripened or had not even been planted, and, in consequence, the numerous bodies of returning soldiers, straggling along the public roads, could find but little to eat. Whatever they were able to pick up was obtained by side excursions that only served to increase the fatigue of their long journey.

It was not long before several thousand men, who had, for many months, been enduring all the hardships of positive hunger, had congregated in Danville as one of the stages in their journey southward. That town, being at a distance from the scenes of the campaigns in Virginia and the West, had become, as has been already pointed out, a centre for the accumulation of many kinds of supplies. The needs of seven thousand prisoners alone required a large quantity of food and clothing to satisfy. Report, naturally enough when men were feeling the pinch of starvation, exaggerated the volume of stores that were lying behind the walls of the Government warehouses. Did not all know that, so far as Virginia at least was concerned, the Confederacy was now entirely defunct? Had not its representative, at the head of an armed detachment, endeavored, a few days before, in obedience to his orders, to destroy these stores by the use of the torch? If left untouched, would they not be soon seized by the Federal advance guard and consumed by the Federal soldiers and the released Federal prisoners?

"We are hungry, we are in tatters," was the cry of the disbanded soldiers. "This food, these clothes, are as much ours as anybody's at this moment. We need them, and we propose to take them. There is nobody who has any right to stand in our way."

Now it happened that the families that inhabited the surrounding country had suffered, during the previous winter, almost as many hardships as the soldiers in the ranks. They had known what it was to be gnawed by a hunger which they were unable to appease owing to the impoverishment of their own larders. Many forms of food, common enough before the war, had long ago entirely vanished, and it had been a frequent experience with all to lack at times even cornbread and meat. Nor were they in a better condition as to clothes; all that they possessed had been manufactured by their own hands out of the coarsest home-produced material. Want had stared at them from their own door sills, and it was doing so at the hour of the Confederacy's collapse more sinisterly than at any previous moment. They too had heard the exaggerated rumors touching the contents of the Danville warehouses, and so they determined that they would go to town in a body and share in the expected distribution. On their arrival there, they at once fraternized with the famished soldiery and accompanied them from warehouse to warehouse.

"This one," they said, "is full of shoes. You have only to break in the doors to obtain all that you need to cover your half naked feet. That warehouse across the street is full of clothes. You can find there all the coats and trousers you require. The warehouse beyond that one is full of meat and flour. There is enough there to satisfy the appetite of a small army."

Was it singular, that, under such seductive guidance, the soldiers, egged on also by their own urgent needs, should have begun to batter in the doors? which were to open up such abundance? But when they had staved in the thick panels, they found the interiors of the storehouses either entirely empty or filled with articles that would neither satisfy their hunger nor clothe their bodies.

Disappointment caused the demoralization to spread. There

was now danger that the private homes would be invaded, their furniture damaged in the confusion, the wardrobes rifled, the supplies of food consumed, and the families terrified. The Mayor, very much alarmed, summoned the town Council to meet at once. The first question considered was: should Colonel Withers be asked to put himself at the head of the community and restore order? He was known to be a man of extraordinary firmness and courage, and all minds turned to him instinctively. But it was suggested that, should he be given absolute power, he would certainly declare martial law and every citizen would be compelled by him to do guard duty. The council broke up after adopting only one measure of defense – the police force of the town was to be immediately increased.

By the following morning, the spirit of disorder had become more rampant because the pangs of hunger had had twelve hours within which to grow sharper. What was simply threatened yesterday by the mob, they now attempted to carry out. When they started off for the private houses in search of the bread, bacon, and sugar which they presumed was to be found in the storerooms, a returned soldier of great size and formidable aspect quickly put himself at their head, and under his leadership, they crowded into the first house and rifled it of every scrap of food which it contained.

News of this action of the mob soon came to Colonel Withers at the Confederate prison. He promptly formed a squad from among the members of the guard, and followed by them, with their guns prepared for instant use, started on the run for the spot. When he arrived there, the leader of the mob had been arrested, and the mob itself dispersed by the Mayor of the town, with the aid of a large body of policemen. But so soon as the disorderly assemblage was broken up in one place, it would come together again in another, with the same threat of rifling the private houses of clothes and food.

Later in the afternoon. Colonel Withers was again hastily summoned. He was informed that several thousand disbanded soldiers, who had just arrived on two trains, were breaking into the

the houses in the vicinity of the station, in their search for something to eat and wear. On reaching the spot, he found to his relief
that they had only entered the Armory and Arsenal; and that they
had done this at the instance of the country people, who had told
them that these buildings contained large quantities of the articles
which were so much desired. But so soon as they had seen that
neither flour, bacon, nor clothes were stored there, they had returned to the station. When Colonel Withers, going among them,
earnestly remonstrated with them for committing such an act of
violence, so foreign to their military record,

"We cannot help it," they replied. "We are really starving.
You can see we are almost in rags. Unless you can persuade the
railway superintendent to forward our trains southward, it will be
impossible to control the men. They must have food, and get it
they will, even if they have to go through the private houses for
it."

"Why don't you dispatch these soldiers' trains right away,"
demanded Colonel Withers of the superintendent, to whose office
he had gone at once.

"The railroad employees are so demoralized," was the
answer, "that they cannot be induced to even pump the water into
the tender. They have pretty well all disappeared."

Colonel Withers returned at once to the station, and
mounting to a platform, which brought him into the full view of
the great throng of soldiers, cried out at the top of his voice, "Attention! Who will come forward to pump water for the engine?"

Several men immediately spoke up. "We started to pump,
but just as soon as we began, the crowd rushed into the cars, and
when we saw that no room would be left for us, we stopped."

"I will post guards at the door of each car," replied Colonel Withers, "and not a man shall be allowed to enter until you
have finished pumping and been admitted to your seats."

The tank was soon full of water; the men who had pumped
it in walked into the cars ahead of their comrades; the engineer got
up steam; and the train fairly bursting with its bronzed, tattered,
half-starving passengers rolled slowly away southward. At once.

Colonel Withers directed his attention to starting the second train, but while he was so engaged, a loud explosion occurred, followed by others in rapid succession. Immediately, the country people, who had collected in large numbers on the outskirts of the crowd of soldiers still occupying the station, raised the cry: "The Yankees have come. They are shelling the town, they are shelling the town. Run, run."

The rustics took to their heels; nor did they pause until they had gone far on the road to their rural homes – a fortunate riddance, as they had, during two days, been solely employed in egging on the soldiery in their search for food and clothing which did not exist. The explosion had really taken place at the Arsenal. That building was full of shells, cartridges, and other munitions, and as the separate stores caught on fire in turn, the heavy reports, following at short intervals, caused the impression that both cannon and musketry had been used in an attack on the town. When the soldiers, finding no food or clothing in the Arsenal, had abandoned it, a band of boys and young men had crept inside to obtain powder and firearms, and, while engaged in rummaging about among the piles, had dropped a match or cigar, which had caused the series of explosions. Not one escaped alive in the destruction which ensued.

So great was the confusion that now prevailed in all parts of the town, and so general was the alarm felt by the citizens, that there was an urgent demand for another meeting of the council and the adoption of the sternest methods for enforcing public order. The council assembled and at once decided to request Colonel Withers to take absolute control over the entire community as the only course that seemed to offer the smallest protection to life and property. The autocratic trust was immediately accepted, and so energetically did he act that, within a few hours, he had organized all the men and youths, from the age of sixteen to that of fifty, into squads of twenty; and at each ferry, ford, and bridge leading into the town from the country on the riverside, and at the head of each street on the open rural side, he stationed one of these squads, with orders to bar the entrance of every human being who might attempt to come in.

It was a wise precaution, for only a short time after these guards were posted, large bands of country people, eager for booty and relieved of all alarm about the supposed bombardment, began to return to the town on foot, horseback, and in farm wagons. They were everywhere halted by the squads, who, lifting their muskets to their shoulders, threatened to shoot the first person who crossed the dead line. Though exposed to a shower of disappointed curses, they held back the excited crowd until the latter perceived that they could not enter the town except by the sacrifice of the lives of hundreds of their own number; and under the influence of this conviction they sullenly turned their faces homeward. The greatest danger that had threatened the community was, by their reluctant retreat, completely averted, for the disbanded soldiers who remained in the town, having never desired to appropriate any articles except food and clothes, which they so sorely needed, were satisfied as far as possible in their wants, and assisted to continue their journey towards their homes.

There was now only one additional peril in sight to be provided against. How was the town to be protected from the depredations of the Federal prisoners, should they succeed in breaking through their walls? There were eight thousand of these men, who had barely kept soul and body together on their short rations, and their humor could not be trusted, should they be able to strike off their shackles. They were now overawed only by small squads of new guards, for the trained ones had gone off with the disbanded Confederate soldiers.

Before this peril could become a reality, the town was confronted by a new and entirely unexpected danger, which had to be promptly faced and removed. It was reported to Colonel Withers that a large body of Federal bummers, who had been hanging on the skirts of the Federal army, were rapidly approaching Danville in open cars propelled by crank or pole over the metals of the railway from Richmond. How was this new peril to be met? If these men were allowed to enter the town, they would commit the very wrongs which had been staved off so successfully during the last few days – they would rob and burn, without the slightest chance of redress on the part of those who suffered. All the trained guards, as we have seen, had departed, and the untrained squads were needed to overawe the prisoners and the country people.

Colonel Withers telegraphed General Wright the character of the situation, but the General, who was expected to pass through Danville on his way to join Sherman in North Carolina, replied that it would be impossible to send any assistance; and that he must take such steps for the protection of the town as he thought proper.

When this non-committal response was received, the bummers were reported to be only twelve miles off. Colonel Withers, not at all discouraged, made up a squad composed entirely of the petty officers who had charge of the guards at the prison, men who had been chosen for that position of extreme responsibility on account of their superior firmness and intelligence. It was just such a body as he needed in this new crisis; and putting himself at their head, he marched them straight to the station, where the bummers were now momentarily expected. The squad numbered only twenty men. Their leader posted them on either side of the track just where it entered the town, in a position to command its length for a considerable distance.

Soon the first car rolled into view. The bummers, who occupied it, held their muskets between their knees as they sat sideways around the platform. They presented a very forbidding and threatening aspect as they were ordered to come to a full stop between the two files.

"Throw down your arms," cried out Colonel Withers, "or you are dead men."

The members of the squad raised their revolvers and took aim.

The bummers, assuming an air of defiance, began to offer a noisy remonstrance at such interference.

"Not one word," exclaimed Colonel Withers. "Throw down your arms and surrender or your lives are the forfeit."

There was no mistaking the meaning of either the language or the attitude of this tall determined man in Confederate uniform. The bummers sullenly gave up their muskets, and under the pistol muzzles of a couple of the squad, were marched off to the prison.

Hardly had they vanished down the nearest street when another car rolled in. The second company of bummers were arrested and subdued in the same resolute manner as the first, and followed their comrades to the prison. A third and fourth car appeared, and the passengers of each in their turn had the like history. Eighty bummers were soon cooling their heels under the ceiling of the same large apartment. Colonel Withers, who had remained at the station until convinced that the last car had come in, returned to the prison, and at once went to the room which was occupied by his latest captives.

"What right have you to detain us," they exclaimed, with an angry shout, as he entered, "the war is over."

"I arrested you for your own sakes," he calmly replied. "You are not safe in this town. If I were to set you free, many of you and many of our citizens would be killed."

Then turning to one among them who seemed to exercise some authority over them all, he said, "General Wright telegraphs me that he will be here tomorrow with his troops. I know you would rather see the devil than to be turned over to him. Now if you will agree to remain quietly in the guard house tonight, I will guarantee you kind treatment, a good supper, and a release tomorrow morning early enough for you to leave town before the General arrives."

They consented, although with undisguised reluctance, to this arrangement, which was afterwards strictly carried out by Colonel Withers. He induced some of his friends among the town people to cook an excellent supper for his captives; they were made comfortable for the night under a strong guard; and next morning, when General Wright was announced to be within a mile of Danville, they were released. They had vehemently demanded their freedom at dawn, but as they were suspected of an intention to commit as many depredations as possible in the interval of license which this would give them, their request was promptly and positively refused.

When the advance body of the Federal troops appeared. Colonel Withers and one of his officers bearing a flag of truce met them at the bridge which led into the town. They were received with courtesy by the commander, but were ordered to return to their quarters. It was with a feeling of relief that Colonel Withers obeyed, for at last all responsibility for the prisoners was shifted from his shoulders. With the presence of Federal soldiers in the town, the danger of the captives running amuck when released was removed.

An hour passed, and General Wright entered Colonel Withers's office at the prison.

"I understand. Colonel," he said, "that you have about one hundred of my men in custody in your guard house."

"A mistake. General. I have no one in the guard house now."

"Strange. I heard it as I thought from a reliable source."

"Well, General, I did have them there last night, but I turned them loose this morning."

"What did you do that for? I would have supposed an officer of your rank would have had no sympathy with such a lot of bummers. I would have given anything in reason to have got hold of them."

"I too would have been glad, as I had not the slightest desire to shield them. You advised me to do the best I could, and I did so. As they kept their part of the bargain, I was bound to keep mine."

A provost-marshal was at once appointed to take charge of the town, and within a few hours, the many thousand prisoners were set free. No disorder, no indulgence in excesses of any kind, followed their release. They remained in the vicinity until trains were brought up to afford them a passage to their homes in the North.

Colonel Withers had saved Danville from the looting country people, from the famished Confederate soldiers, from the ma-

rauding Federal bummers, and finally from the possible depredations of thousands of hungry and angry captives. Determination,
firmness, courage, promptness – these were the great qualities
which he had shown in the difficult and perplexing situation in
which he was placed, and they entitled him to as much honor as
the coolness and bravery which he had always displayed on the
field of battle.

www.ingramcontent.com/pod-product-compliance
Lightning Source LLC
Chambersburg PA
CBHW071421090426
42737CB00011B/1530